PHILIP
GLASS

KNEE PLAYS 1-5

FROM *EINSTEIN ON THE BEACH*

STUDY SCORE

CHESTER MUSIC

DU10901

ISBN 978-1-78038-678-2

Cover image: Knee Play 4 from the Robert Wilson
production of *Einstein on the Beach*
photo © Lucie Jansch

Music engraving by Jon Bunker

Published in Great Britain by Chester Music Limited
Head office:
14-15, Berners Street,
London W1T 3LJ

Sales and hire:
Music Sales Distribution Centre,
Newmarket Road,
Bury St. Edmunds,
Suffolk IP33 3YB,

www.chesternovello.com

Printed in the EU

Individual *Knee Play* titles are available as follows:

Knee Play 1 (SATB and organ)	DU10627
Knee Play 2 (solo violin)	DU10659
Knee Play 3 (SATB unaccompanied)	DU10626
Knee Play 4 (TB and solo violin)	DU10670 (violin part DU10670-01)
Knee Play 5 (SA, solo violin and organ)	DU10671 (violin part DU10671-01)

CONTENTS

PHILIP GLASS: THE "KNEE PLAYS" FROM *EINSTEIN ON THE BEACH*

Since its first performance at the Avignon Festival in 1976, Robert Wilson and Philip Glass's *Einstein on the Beach* has passed into both theatrical and musical history. Lasting some five-and-a-half hours, the work - in addition to a violinist representing Albert Einstein himself, dressed as in a famous photograph of him (the scientist was a keen amateur violin player) - involves singers both solo and choral, actors, dancers and the composer's own amplified ensemble.

Redefining "opera", *Einstein* avoids both any conventional narrative and any straightforward representation of the characters it features. These do, nevertheless, as we have seen, include Einstein, discoverer of relativity. A number of other things that we see are, indeed, also fairly readily explained: a train, for instance, which evidently references relativity as it does in many scientific accounts. Yet the work is still a new kind of "theatre of images"[1] in which texts are spoken, not sung, and the singers chant numbers and *solfège* syllables; in which the music, though typically minimalist in Glass's style of the early 1970s, is wide-ranging in manner, some of it excitingly dramatic, some of it heart-achingly lyrical; and in which dance, sets and lighting are all central to the drama. *Einstein's* reconfiguration of the functions of, and the relationships between, spectacle, text, dance and music has become a touchstone of downtown mixed media, alternative theatre, musical minimalism and much else besides.

The "Knee Plays" are officially *Einstein's* prologue, interludes and epilogue; all are enacted in the right-hand corner of the stage space near the audience. Their five scenes - interspersed before, between and after the work's four acts, with their unstable and evolving images of train, trial and field (the latter not as in "farm" but as in Einstein's "unified field theory") - are, at mostly between six and eight minutes each, shorter than any of the official main scenes within those acts.

Yet the importance of these Knee Plays is far greater than this apparently subsidiary role suggests. Their curious name derives from this linking function: "the 'knee'," writes Glass, "referring to the joining function that humans' anatomical knees perform". Any attempt to say what the Knee Plays are about is ultimately as difficult as defining the meaning of the work of which they form part. We can, though, confidently say that three of them - nos. 2, 4 and 5 - involve the solo violinist as *Einstein*, sitting halfway between the stage and the orchestra pit.

Knee Play 1, based on a VI-V-I cadence in C major – initially with just the bass line already playing, over and over again for around fifteen minutes, by an electric organ as the audience enters - combines numbers, both sung and spoken, sung *solfège* and spoken texts by Christopher Knowles (a brain-damaged boy whom Wilson involved extensively in Einstein). Two female actor/dancers sit at small tables for the first two Knee Plays; the chorus of sixteen mixed voices have filed one by one into the orchestra pit before the main part of Knee Play 1 begins.

Knee Plays 2, 3 and 4 are all based on different versions of the chromatic five-chord cadential pattern that its composer calls "the most prominent 'theme' of the

opera". Nos. 3 and 4 also incorporate variants of Knee Play 1's VI-V-I cadence. Knee Play 2 counterpoints a violin line of A-minor scales and different versions of the five-chord cadential pattern against sequences of numbers and texts similar to those of Knee Play 1 (plus, on the work's 1993 recording, a sung drone for a while), this time just with two actors and no chorus.

Knee Play 3 is for unaccompanied chorus, alternating vigorously chanted number sequences with lyrically sung *solfège*. Their pit placement doesn't prevent them here from suddenly flourishing toothbrushes or mimicking Einstein in another famous photograph, sticking out his tongue. The two actors, though, are now only standing by in silence. Knee Play 4 is for male chorus and violin: another alternation, in both harmony and mood, but less sharply contrasted this time and using only *solfège*. Here, the two solo stage performers of Knee Plays 1-3 twist and turn on glass tables lit from beneath.

Knee Play 5 - occurring after the general mayhem of Wilson's representation not merely of space flight but also of nuclear holocaust in the "Spaceship" scene of Act 4 - returns to the musical materials, chanted numbers, sung *solfège* and original spoken text of Knee Play 1, once more built entirely on the VI-V-I cadence. This time around, however, at least in the original production and the two existing commercial recordings, Samuel M. Johnson (an elderly retired actor who had become another crucial member of Wilson's cast of creator-characters) read his own text, "Lovers on a Park Bench" (represented by the pair of female performers who have appeared in every Knee Play), to bring this epic to a rapt, magical - and rather surprising - conclusion.

Keith Potter

---

[1]Philip Glass, ed. Robert T. Jones, *Opera on the Beach* (London and Boston: Faber, 1988), p. 7.

Knee Play 1

Philip Glass

3
S
A
1 2 3 4 2 3 4 5 6 1 2 3 4 5 6 7 8
T
B
Org.
4
S
A
2 3 4 1 2 3 4 5 6 1 2 3 4 5 6 7 8
T
B
Org.
5
S
A
2 3 4 1 2 3 4 5 6 2 3 4 5 6 7 8
T
B
Org.
6
S
A
1 2 3 4 1 2 3 4 5 6 2 3 4 5 6 7 8
T
B
Org.

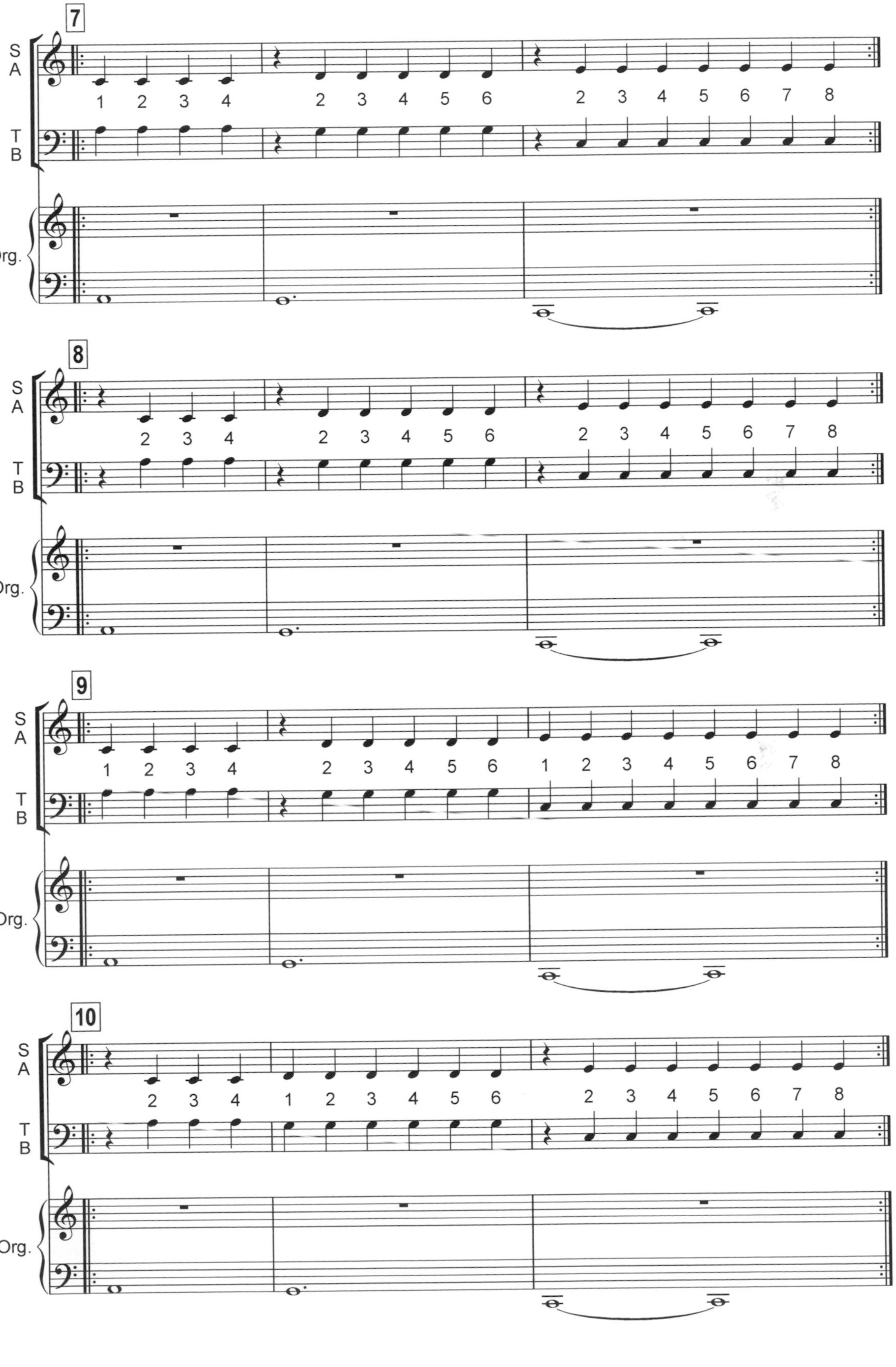
7
S
A
1 2 3 4 2 3 4 5 6 2 3 4 5 6 7 8
T
B
Org.
8
S
A
2 3 4 2 3 4 5 6 2 3 4 5 6 7 8
T
B
Org.
9
S
A
1 2 3 4 2 3 4 5 6 1 2 3 4 5 6 7 8
T
B
Org.
10
S
A
2 3 4 1 2 3 4 5 6 2 3 4 5 6 7 8
T
B
Org.

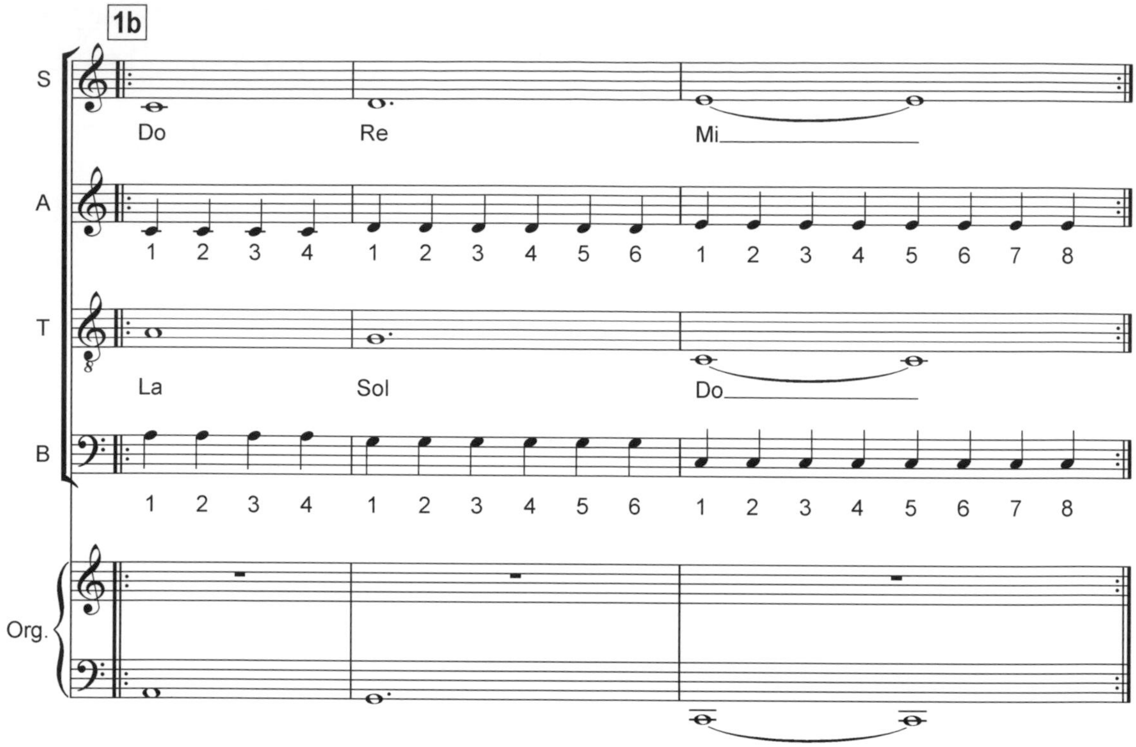
1b
S
A
T
B
Org.
Do
Re
Mi
1 2 3 4 1 2 3 4 5 6 1 2 3 4 5 6 7 8
La
Sol
Do
1 2 3 4 1 2 3 4 5 6 1 2 3 4 5 6 7 8

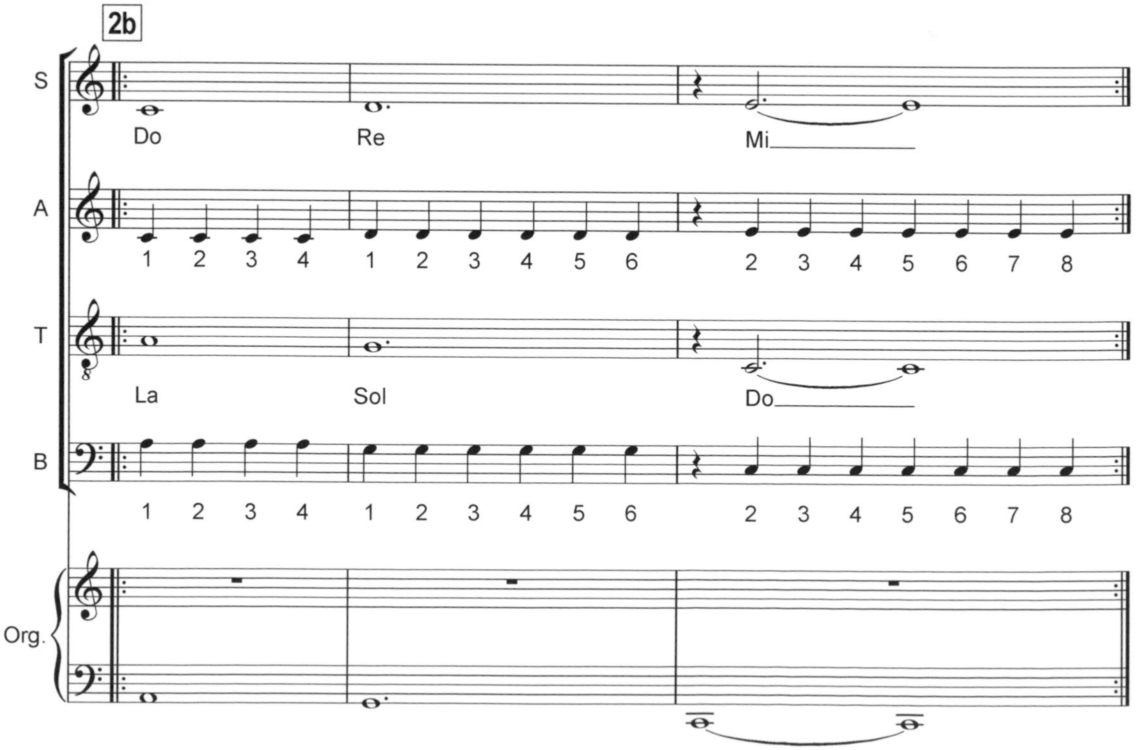
2b
S
A
T
B
Org.
Do
Re
Mi
1 2 3 4 1 2 3 4 5 6 2 3 4 5 6 7 8
La
Sol
Do
1 2 3 4 1 2 3 4 5 6 2 3 4 5 6 7 8

3b
S
Do
Re
Mi
A
1 2 3 4
2 3 4 5 6
1 2 3 4 5 6 7 8
T
La
Sol
Do
B
1 2 3 4
2 3 4 5 6
1 2 3 4 5 6 7 8
Org.

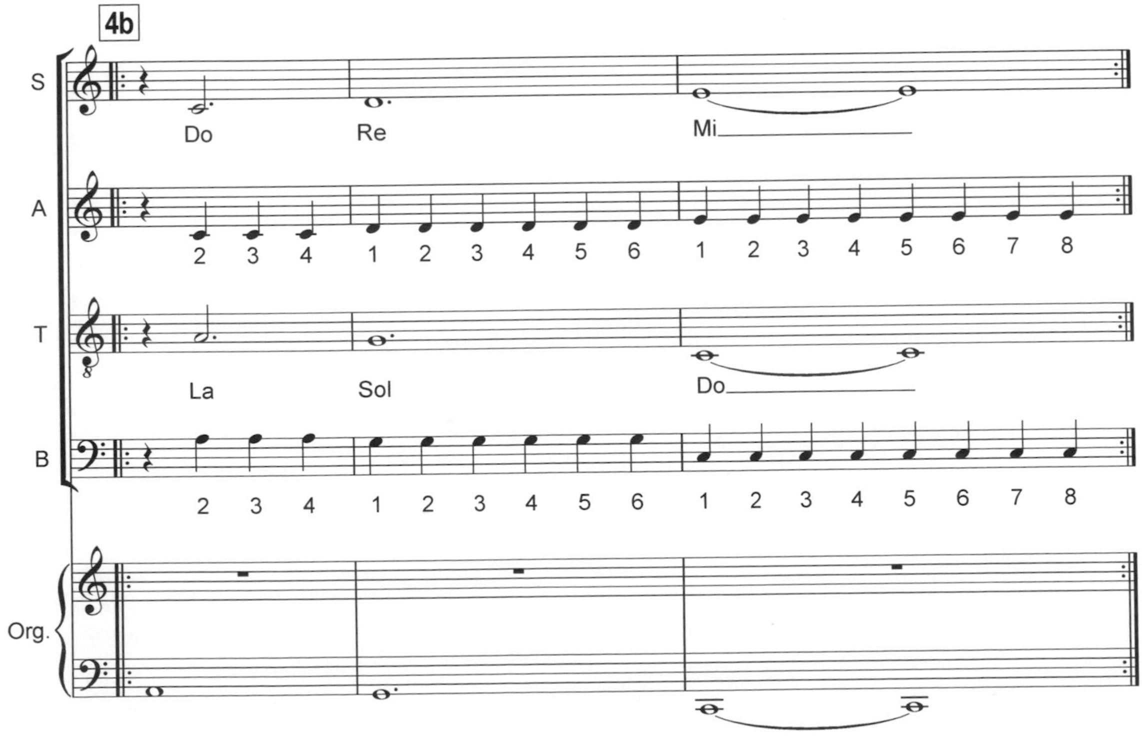
4b
S
Do
Re
Mi
A
2 3 4
1 2 3 4 5 6
1 2 3 4 5 6 7 8
T
La
Sol
Do
B
2 3 4
1 2 3 4 5 6
1 2 3 4 5 6 7 8
Org.

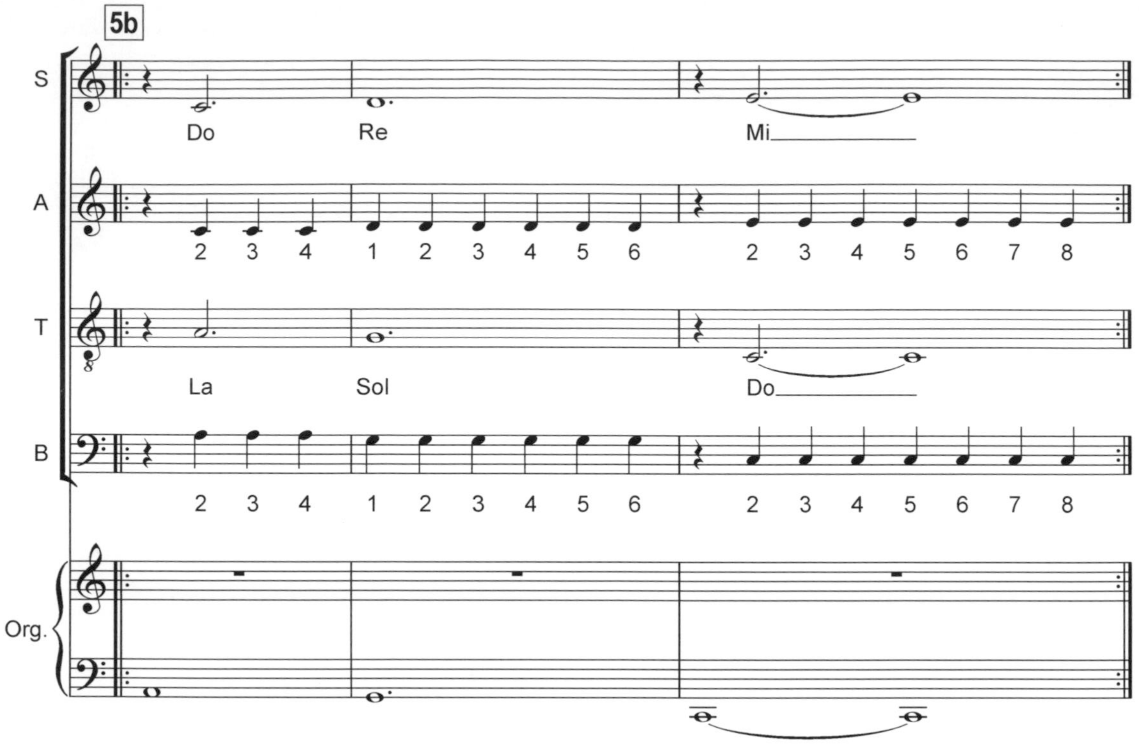
5b
S
Do
Re
Mi
A
2 3 4 1 2 3 4 5 6 2 3 4 5 6 7 8
T
La
Sol
Do
B
2 3 4 1 2 3 4 5 6 2 3 4 5 6 7 8
Org.

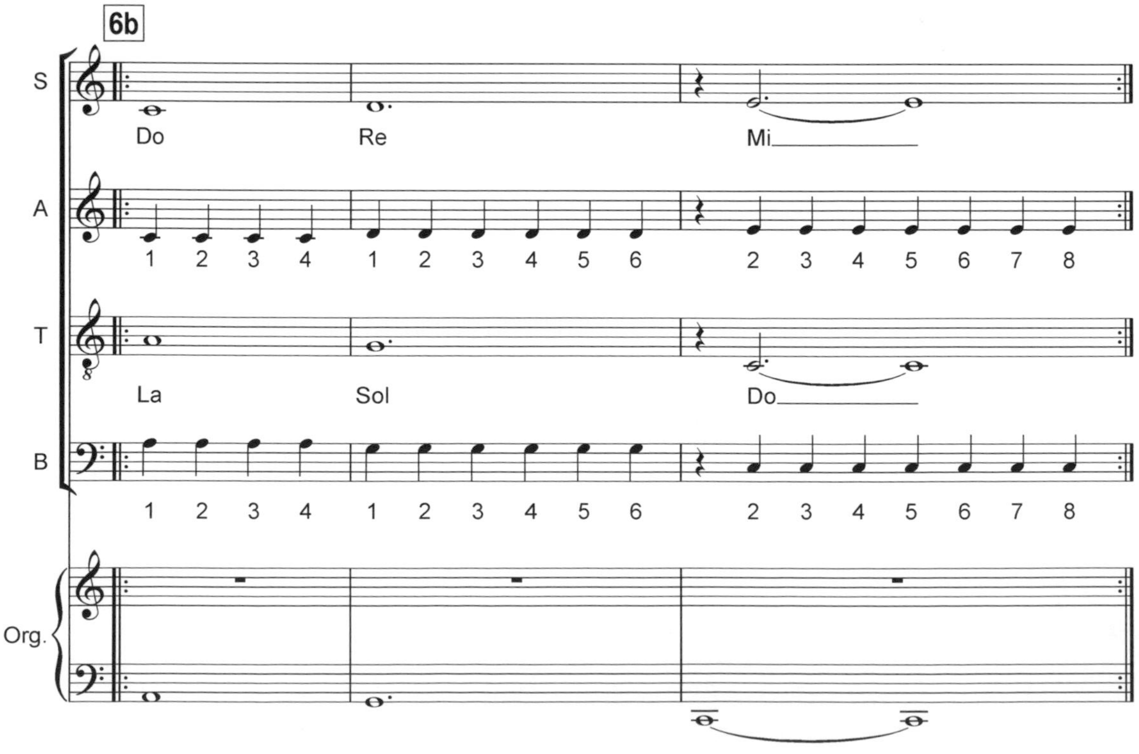
6b
S
Do
Re
Mi
A
1 2 3 4 1 2 3 4 5 6 2 3 4 5 6 7 8
T
La
Sol
Do
B
1 2 3 4 1 2 3 4 5 6 2 3 4 5 6 7 8
Org.

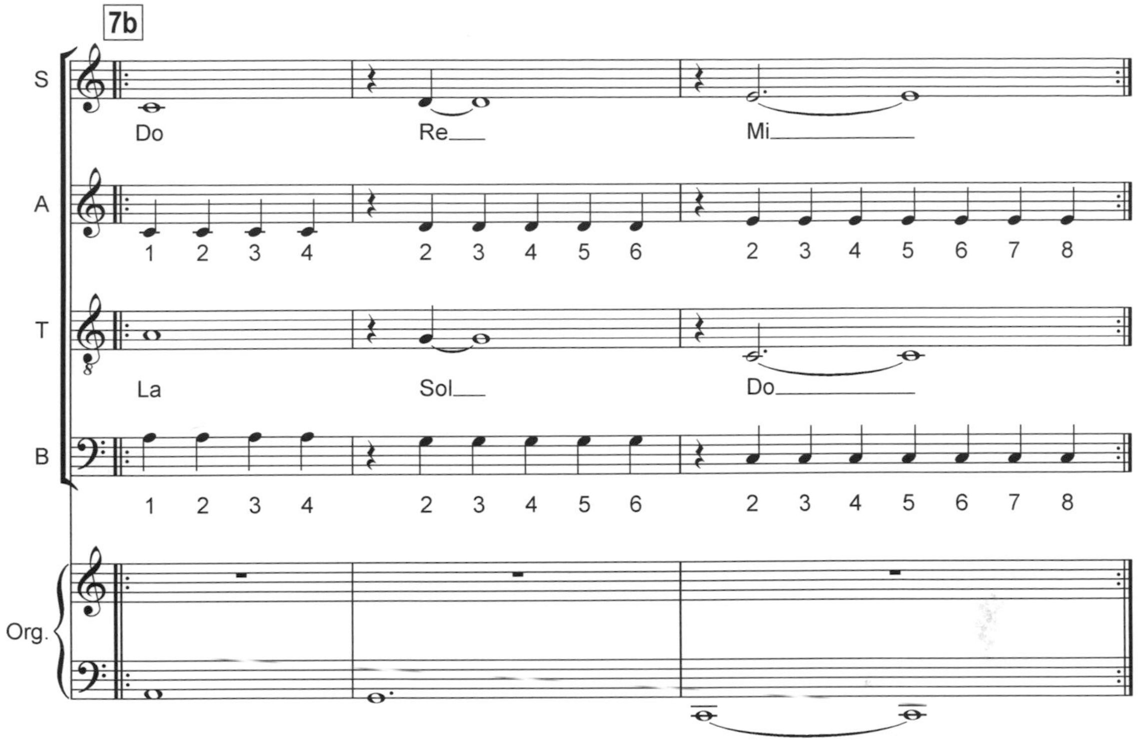
7b
S
Do
Re___
Mi___________
A
1 2 3 4
2 3 4 5 6
2 3 4 5 6 7 8
T
La
Sol___
Do___________
B
1 2 3 4
2 3 4 5 6
2 3 4 5 6 7 8
Org.

8b
S
Do
Re___
Mi___________
A
2 3 4
2 3 4 5 6
2 3 4 5 6 7 8
T
La
Sol___
Do___________
B
2 3 4
2 3 4 5 6
2 3 4 5 6 7 8
Org.

9b

S
Do
Re
Mi
A
1 2 3 4
2 3 4 5 6
1 2 3 4 5 6 7 8
T
La
Sol
Do
B
1 2 3 4
2 3 4 5 6
1 2 3 4 5 6 7 8
Org.

10b

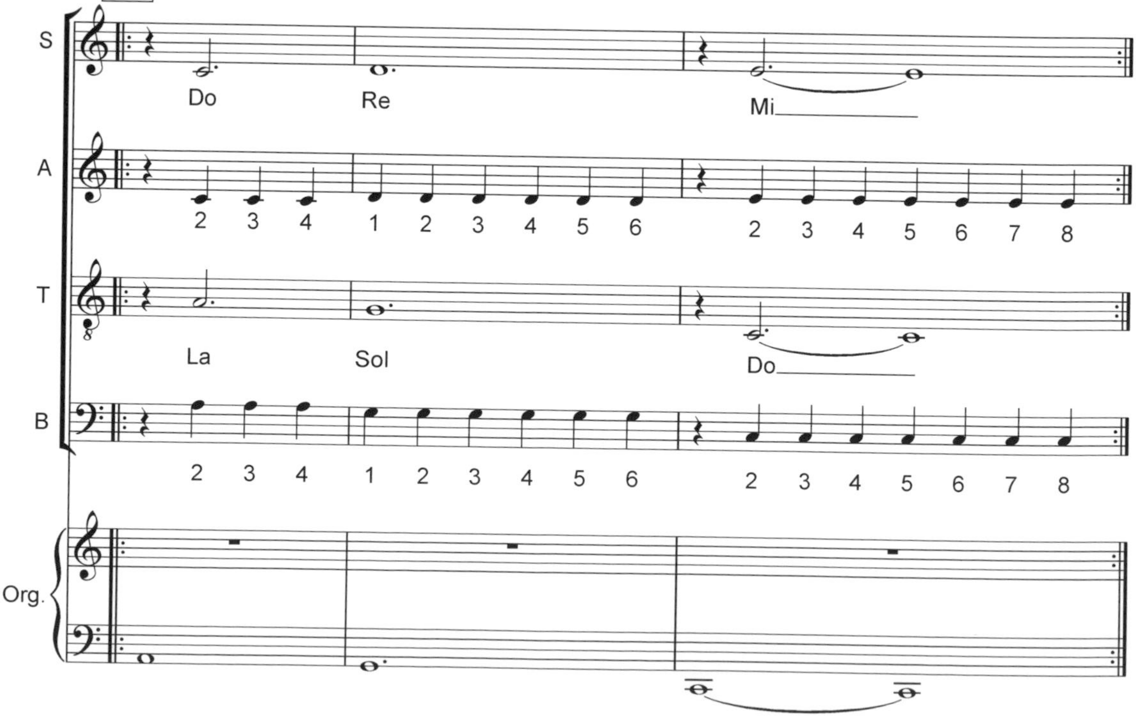
S
Do
Re
Mi
A
2 3 4
1 2 3 4 5 6
2 3 4 5 6 7 8
T
La
Sol
Do
B
2 3 4
1 2 3 4 5 6
2 3 4 5 6 7 8
Org.

KNEE PLAY 2

Philip Glass

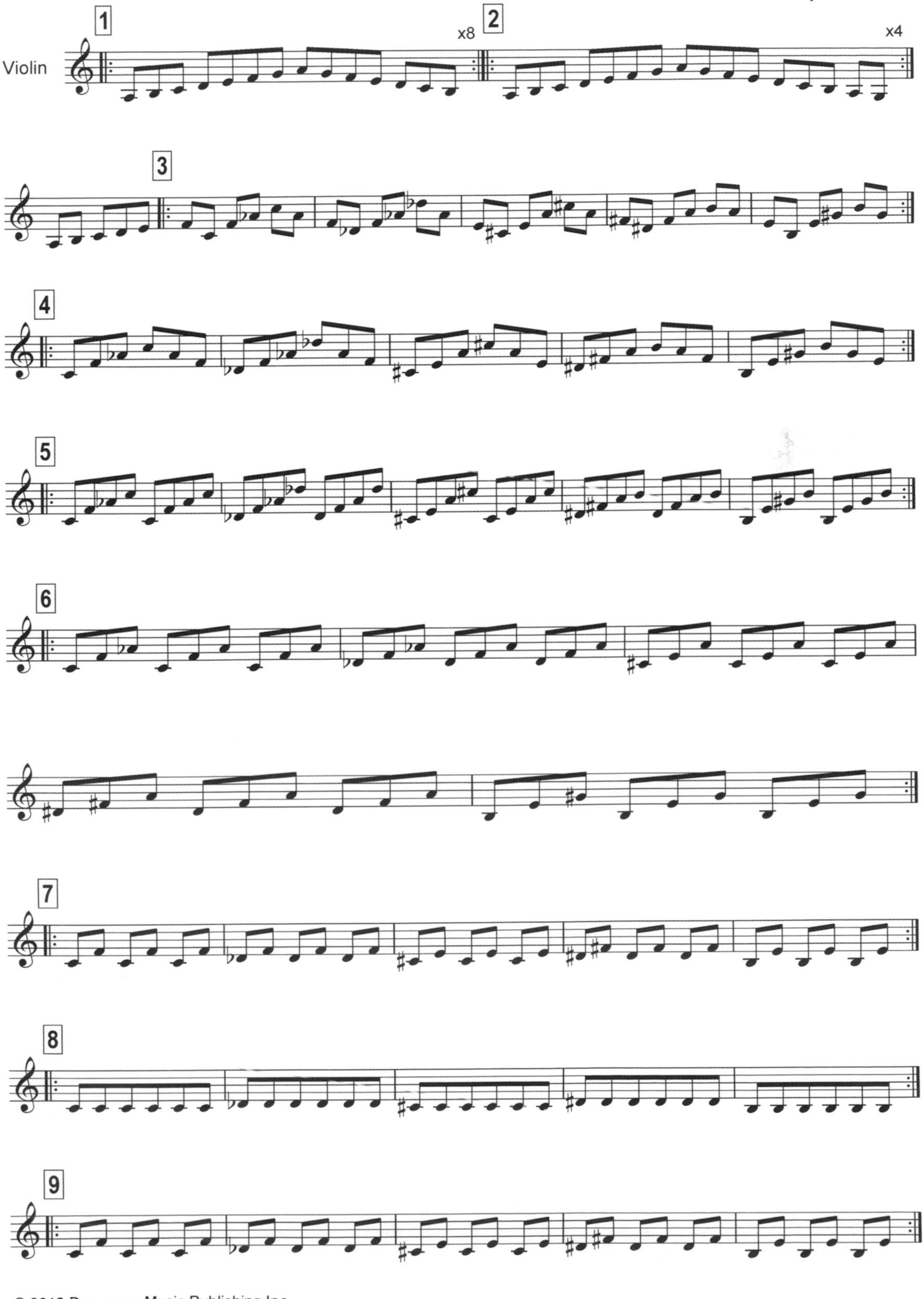

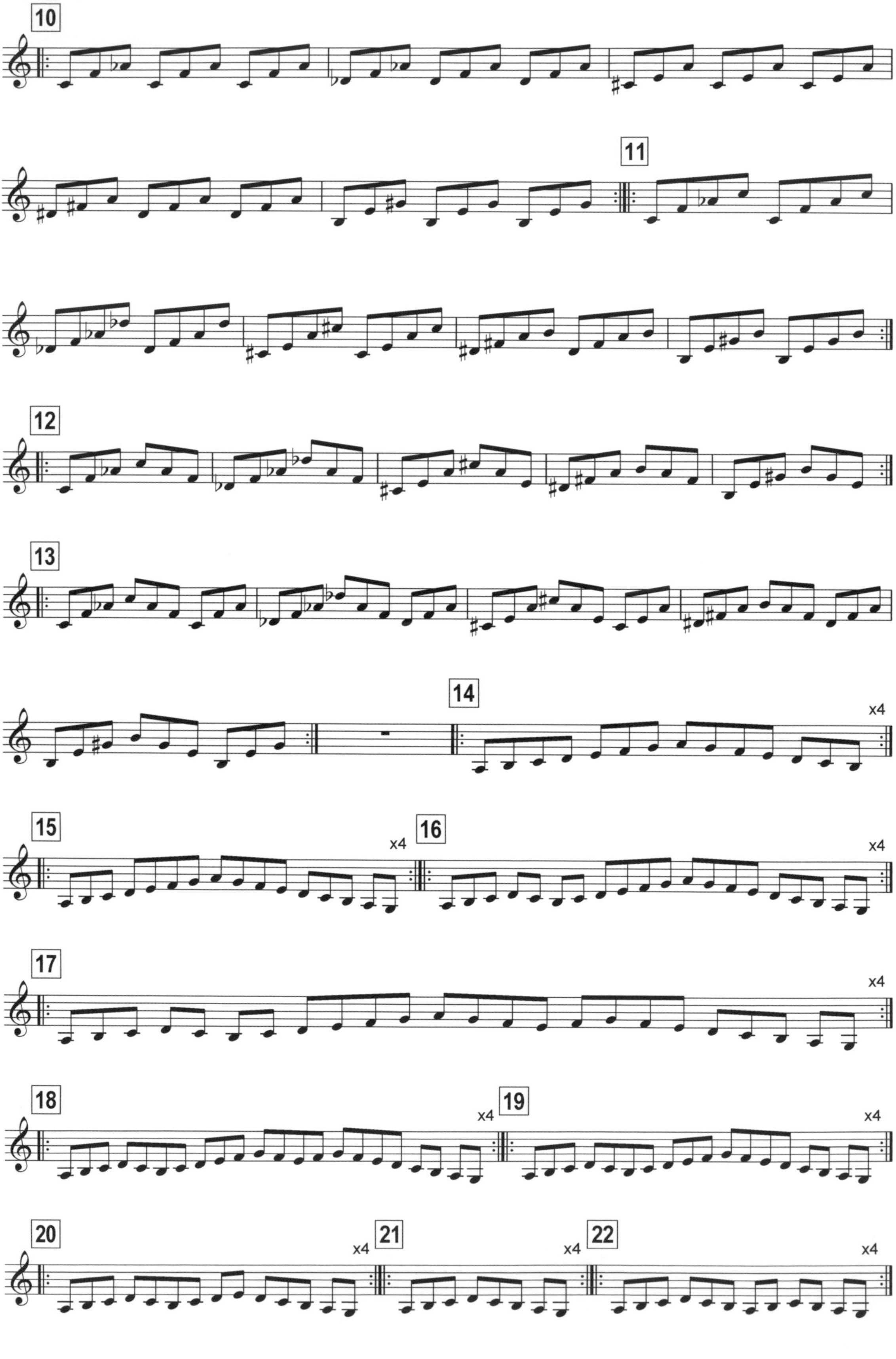
10
11
12
13
14
x4
15
x4
16
x4
17
x4
18
x4
19
x4
20
x4
21
x4
22
x4

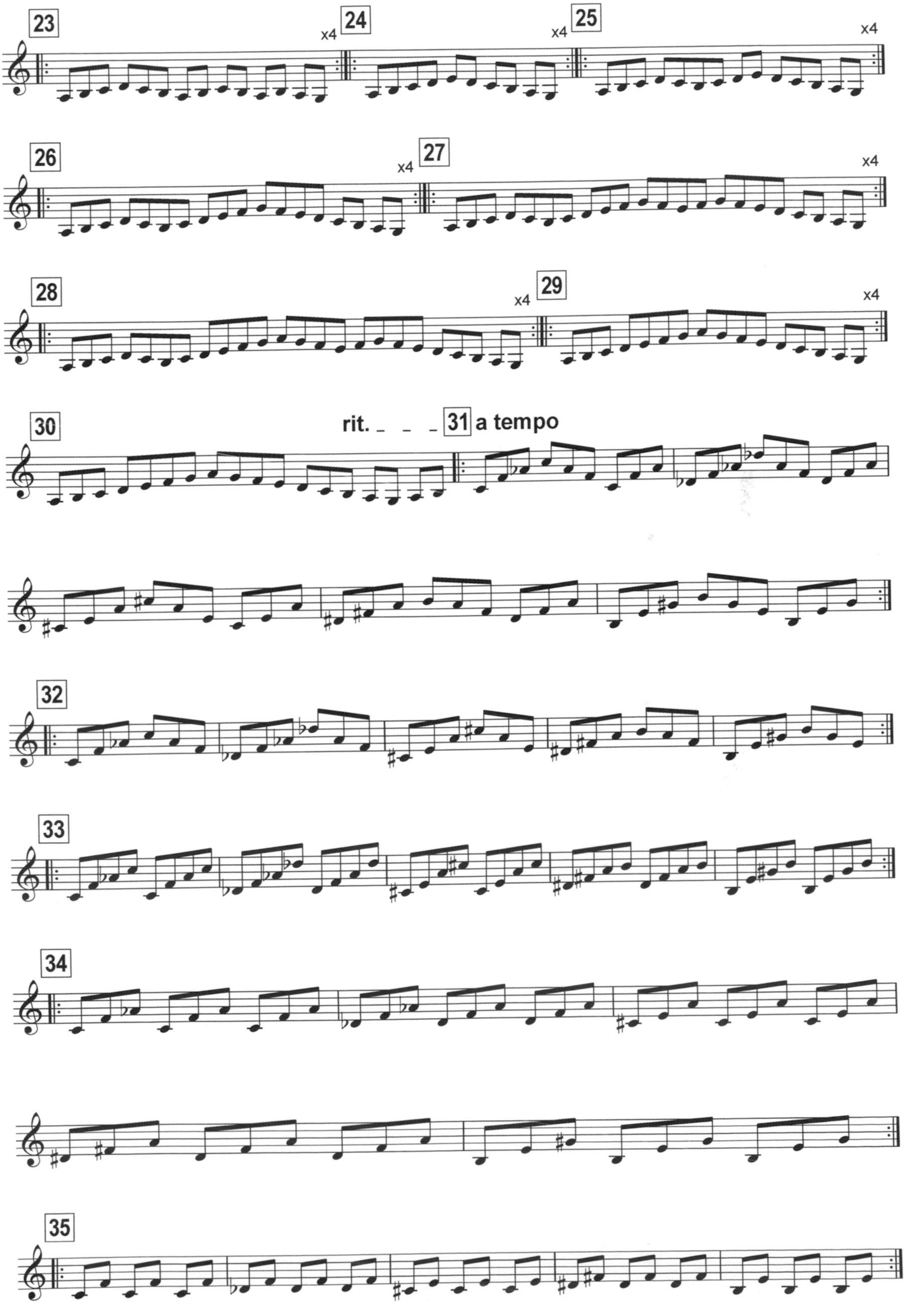
23
x4
24
x4
25
x4
26
x4
27
x4
28
x4
29
x4
30
rit.
31
a tempo
32
33
34
35

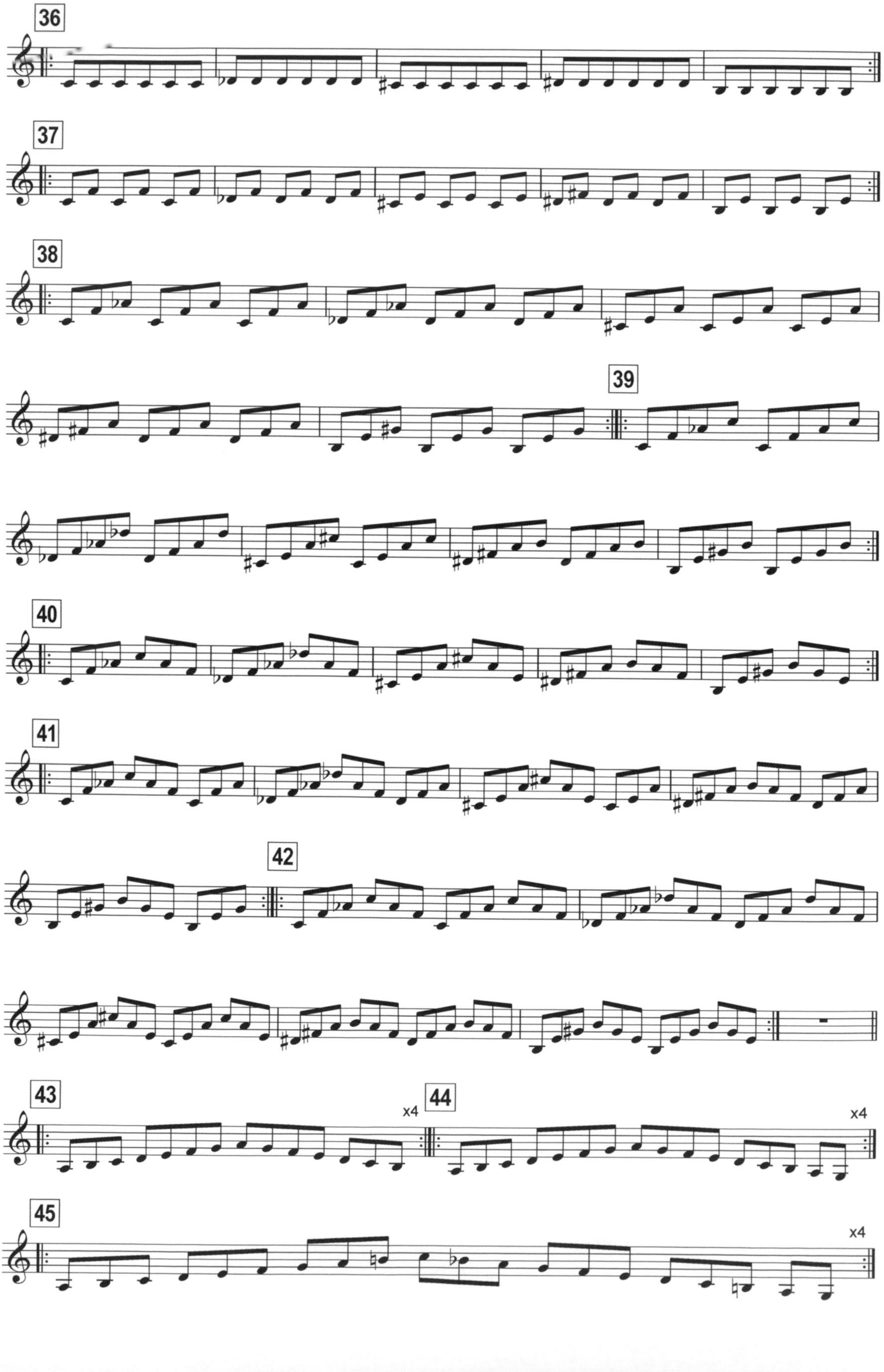
36
37
38
39
40
41
42
43
x4
44
x4
45
x4

Knee Play 3

Philip Glass

3
S
A
1 2 3 1 2 3 1 2 3 1 2 3 1 2 3 1 2 3 1 2 3 1 2 3 1 2 3 1 2 3
T
B
Org.
4
S
A
1 2 3 1 2 3 1 2 3 1 2 1 2 3 1 2 1 2 3 1 2 1 2 3 1 2 1 2 3 1 2
T
B
Org.
5
S
A
1 2 3 1 2 1 2 3 1 2 1 2 3 1 2 1 2 3 1 2 1 2 3 1 2
T
B
Org.

6
S
A
1 2 3 1 2 1 2 3 1 2 1 2 3 1 2 3 1 2 3 1 2 3 1 2 3 1 2 3
T
B
Org.
7
S
A
1 2 3 1 2 3 1 2 3 1 2 3 1 2 3 1 2 3 1 2 3 4 1 2 3 1 2 3 4 1 2 3
T
B
Org.
S
A
1 2 3 4 1 2 3 1 2 3 4 1 2 3 1 2 3 4 1 2 3 1 2 3 4 1 2 3
T
B
Org.

8
S
A
1 2 3 4 1 2 3 4 1 2 3 4 1 2 3 4 1 2 3 4 1 2 3 4
T
B
Org.
S
A
1 2 3 4 1 2 3 4 1 2 3 4 1 2 3 4 1 2 3 4 1 2 3 4
T
B
Org.
9
S
A
1 2 3 4 1 2 3 4 1 2 3 4 1 2 3 4 1 2 3 4 1 2 3 4 1 2 3 4 1 2 3 4
T
B
Org.

10
S
A
1 2 3 4 1 2 3 4 1 2 3 4 1 2 3 4 1 2 3 4 1 2 3 1 2 3 4 1 2 3 1 2 3 4 1 2 3
T
B
Org.
11
S
A
1 2 3 4 1 2 3 1 2 3 4 1 2 3 1 2 3 4 1 2 3 1 2 3 1 2 3
T
B
Org.
S
A
1 2 3 1 2 3 1 2 3 1 2 3 1 2 3 1 2 3 1 2 3 1 2 3 1 2 3 1 2 3
T
B
Org.

12
S
A
1 2 3 1 2 1 2 3 1 2 1 2 3 1 2 1 2 3 1 2
T
B
Org.
13
S
A
1 2 3 1 2 1 2 3 1 2 1 2 3 1 2 3 1 2 3 1 2 3
T
B
Org.
S
A
1 2 3 1 2 3 1 2 3 1 2 3 1 2 3 1 2 3 1 2 3 1 2 3
T
B
12/8
Org.

14
x4
S
Do Re Mi
A
Do Re Do
T
La Do La Do La Do Si Re Si Re Si Re Sol Si Sol Si Sol Si Sol Do Sol Do Sol Do
B
Mi Re Do
x4
Org.

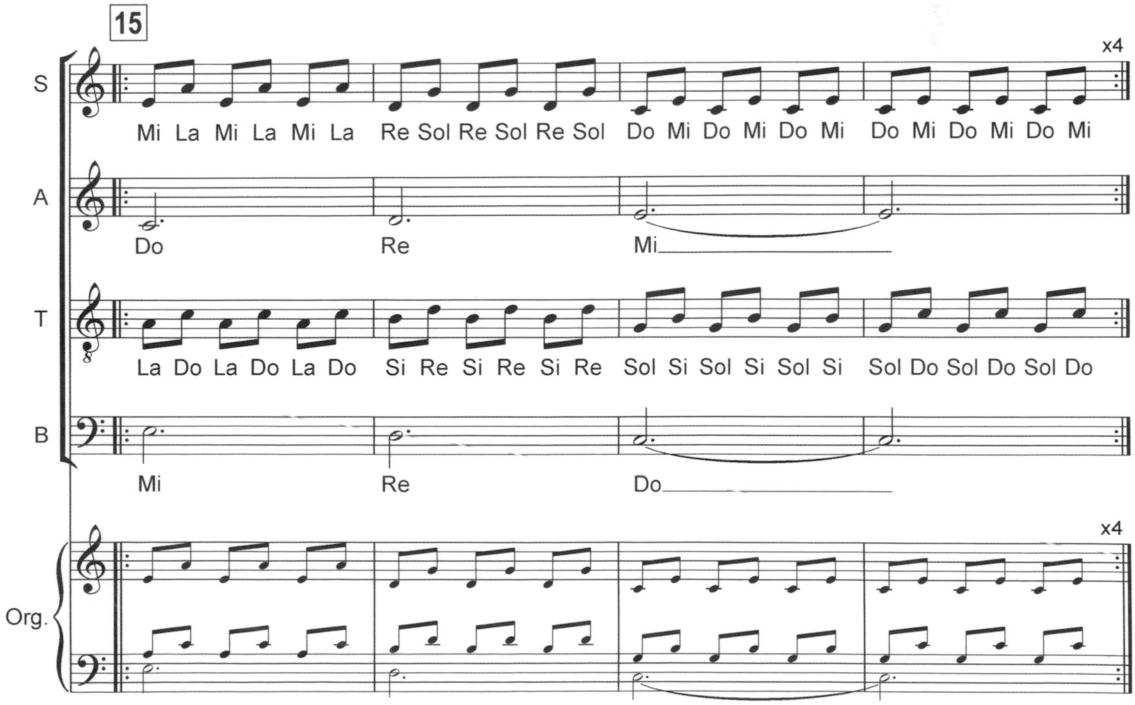
15
x4
S
Mi La Mi La Mi La Re Sol Re Sol Re Sol Do Mi Do Mi Do Mi Do Mi Do Mi Do Mi
A
Do Re Mi
T
La Do La Do La Do Si Re Si Re Si Re Sol Si Sol Si Sol Si Sol Do Sol Do Sol Do
B
Mi Re Do
x4
Org.

16
x4
(x2 on D.S.)
S
Mi La Mi La Mi La Re Sol Re Sol Re Sol Do Mi Do Mi Do Mi Do Mi Do Mi Do Mi
A
Do Mi Do Mi Do Mi Si Re Si Re Si Re Si Do Si Do Si Do Si Do Si Do Si Do
T
La Do La Do La Do Sol Si Sol Si Sol Si Sol Si Sol Si Sol Si Sol Do Sol Do Sol Do
B
Mi Re Do
x4
(x2 on D.S.)
Org.

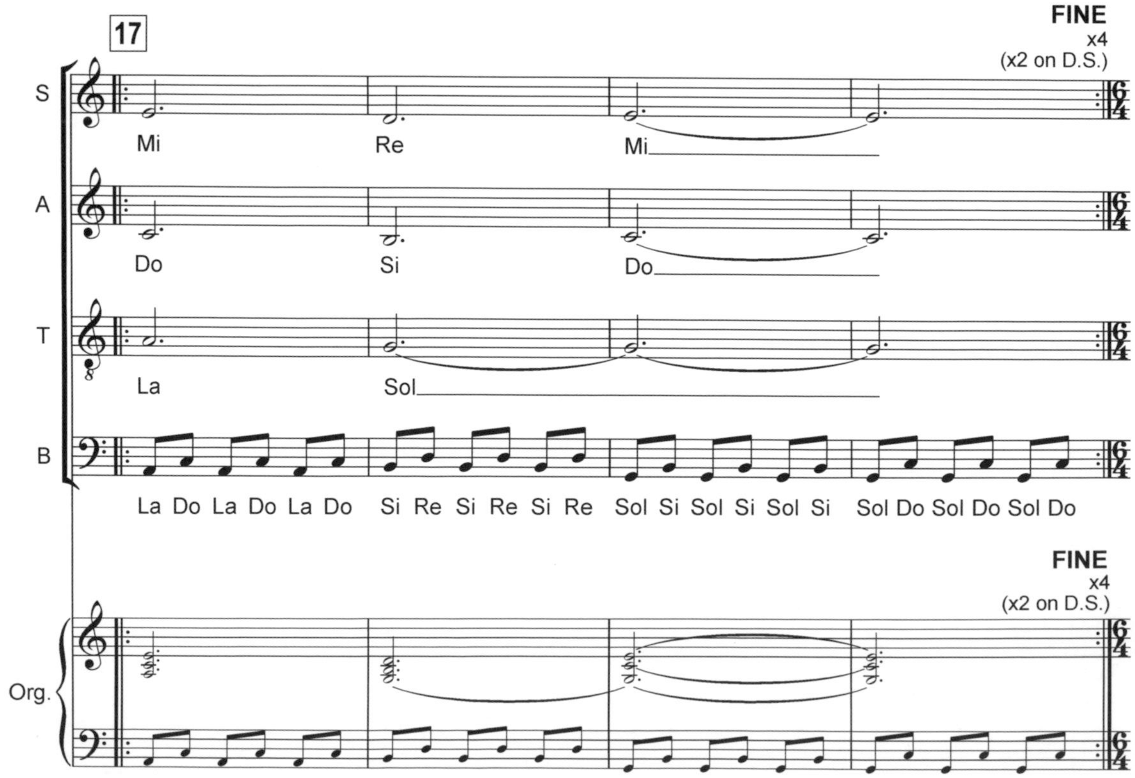
17
FINE
x4
(x2 on D.S.)
S
Mi Re Mi
A
Do Si Do
T
La Sol
B
La Do La Do La Do Si Re Si Re Si Re Sol Si Sol Si Sol Si Sol Do Sol Do Sol Do
FINE
x4
(x2 on D.S.)
Org.

18
S
A
T
B
Org.
1 2 3 1 2 3 1 2 3 1 2 3 1 2 3 1 2 3 1 2 3 1 2 3
19
1 2 3 1 2 3 1 2 3 1 2 3 1 2 3 4 1 2 3 1 2 3 4 1 2 3
1 2 3 4 1 2 3 1 2 3 4 1 2 3 1 2 3 4 1 2 3 1 2 3 4 1 2 3

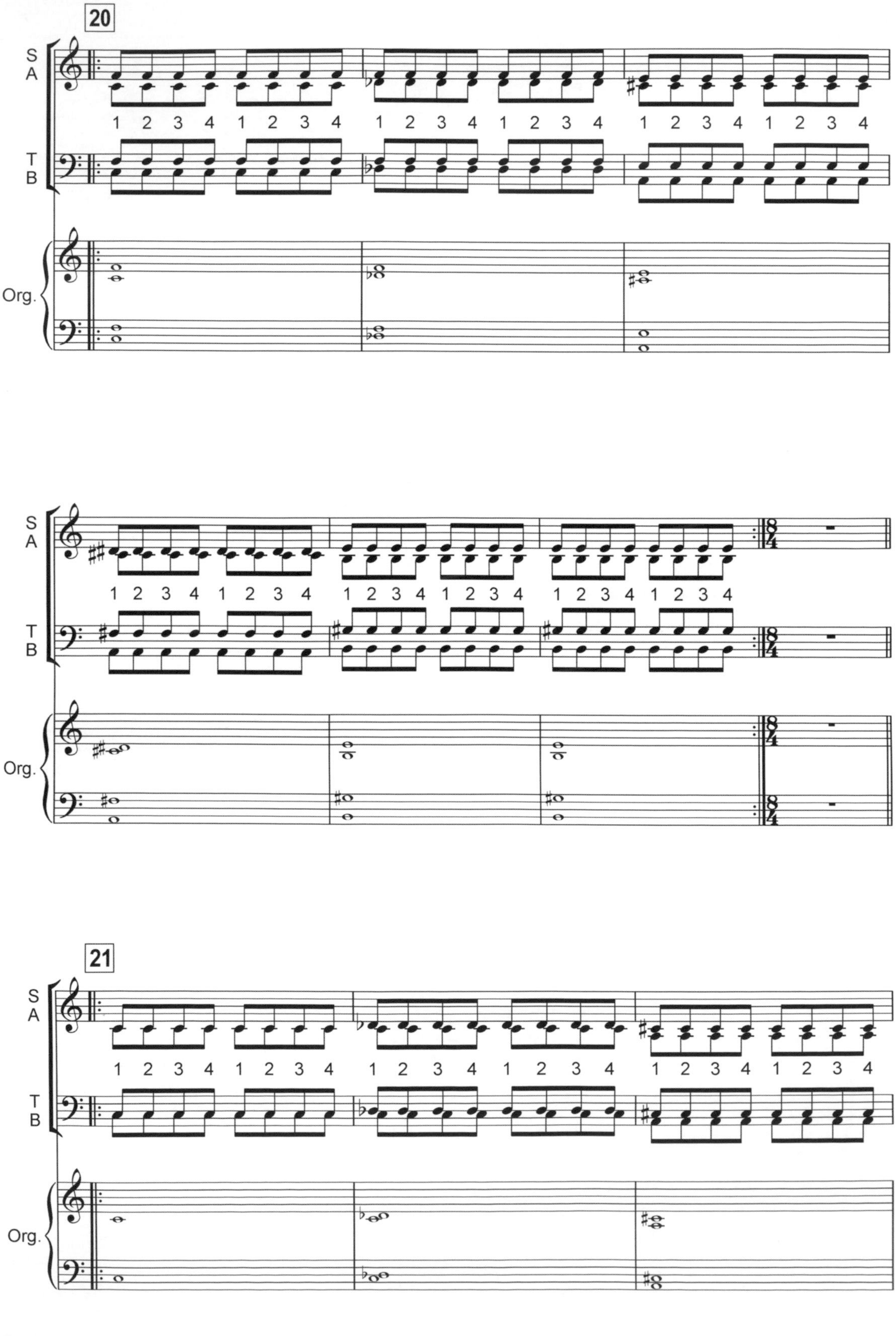
20
S
A
1 2 3 4 1 2 3 4 1 2 3 4 1 2 3 4 1 2 3 4 1 2 3 4
T
B
Org.
S
A
1 2 3 4 1 2 3 4 1 2 3 4 1 2 3 4 1 2 3 4 1 2 3 4
T
B
Org.
21
S
A
1 2 3 4 1 2 3 4 1 2 3 4 1 2 3 4 1 2 3 4 1 2 3 4
T
B
Org.

S
A
1 2 3 4 1 2 3 4 1 2 3 4 1 2 3 4 1 2 3 4 1 2 3 4
T
B
Org.
22
S
A
1 2 3 1 2 3 1 2 3 1 2 3 1 2 3 1 2 3 1 2 3 1 2 3 1 2 3
T
B
Org.
S
A
1 2 3 1 2 3 1 2 3 1 2 3 1 2 3 1 2 3 1 2 3 1 2 3 1 2 3
T
B
Org.

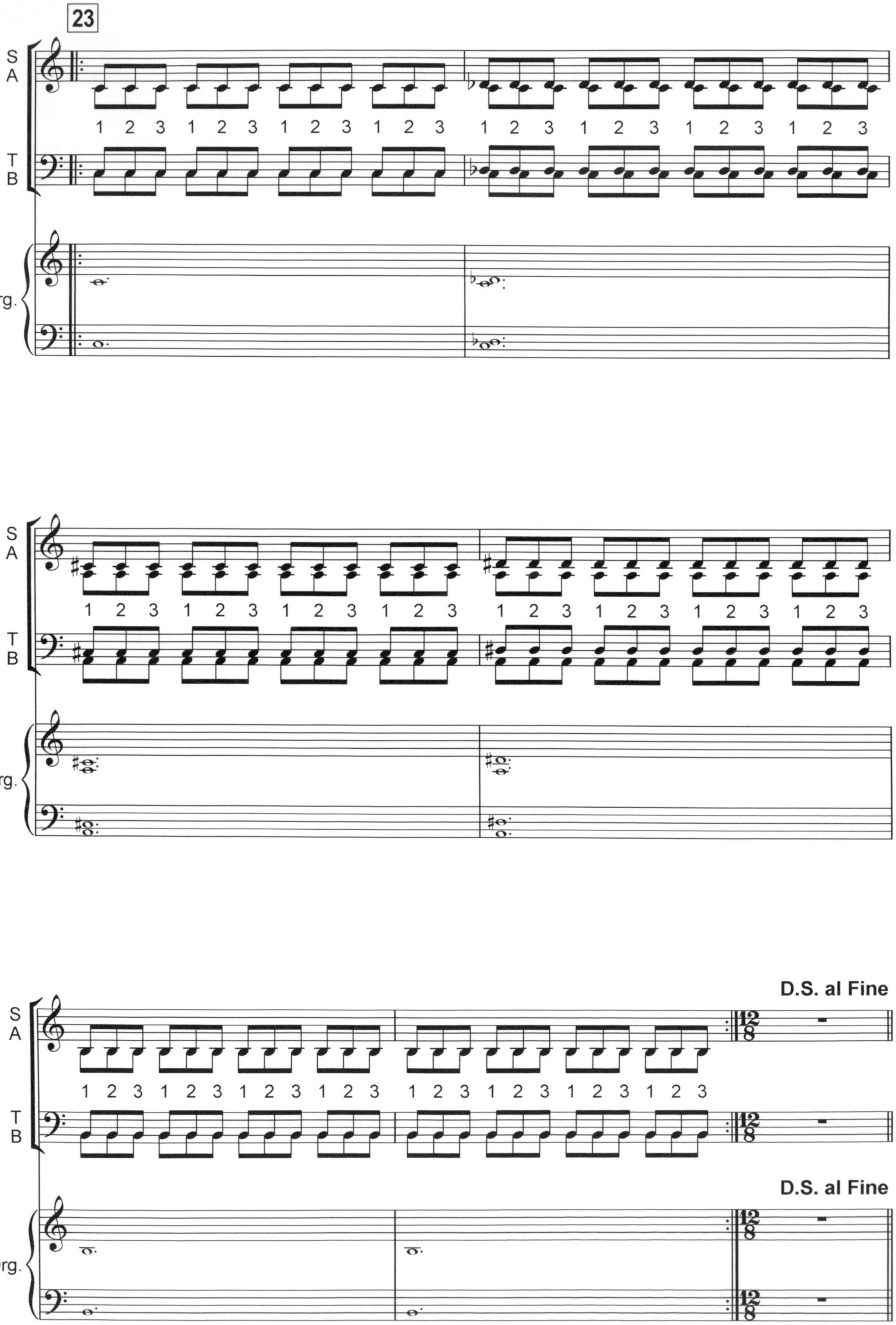
23
S
A
1 2 3 1 2 3 1 2 3 1 2 3 1 2 3 1 2 3 1 2 3 1 2 3
T
B
Org.
D.S. al Fine
D.S. al Fine

Knee Play 4

Philip Glass

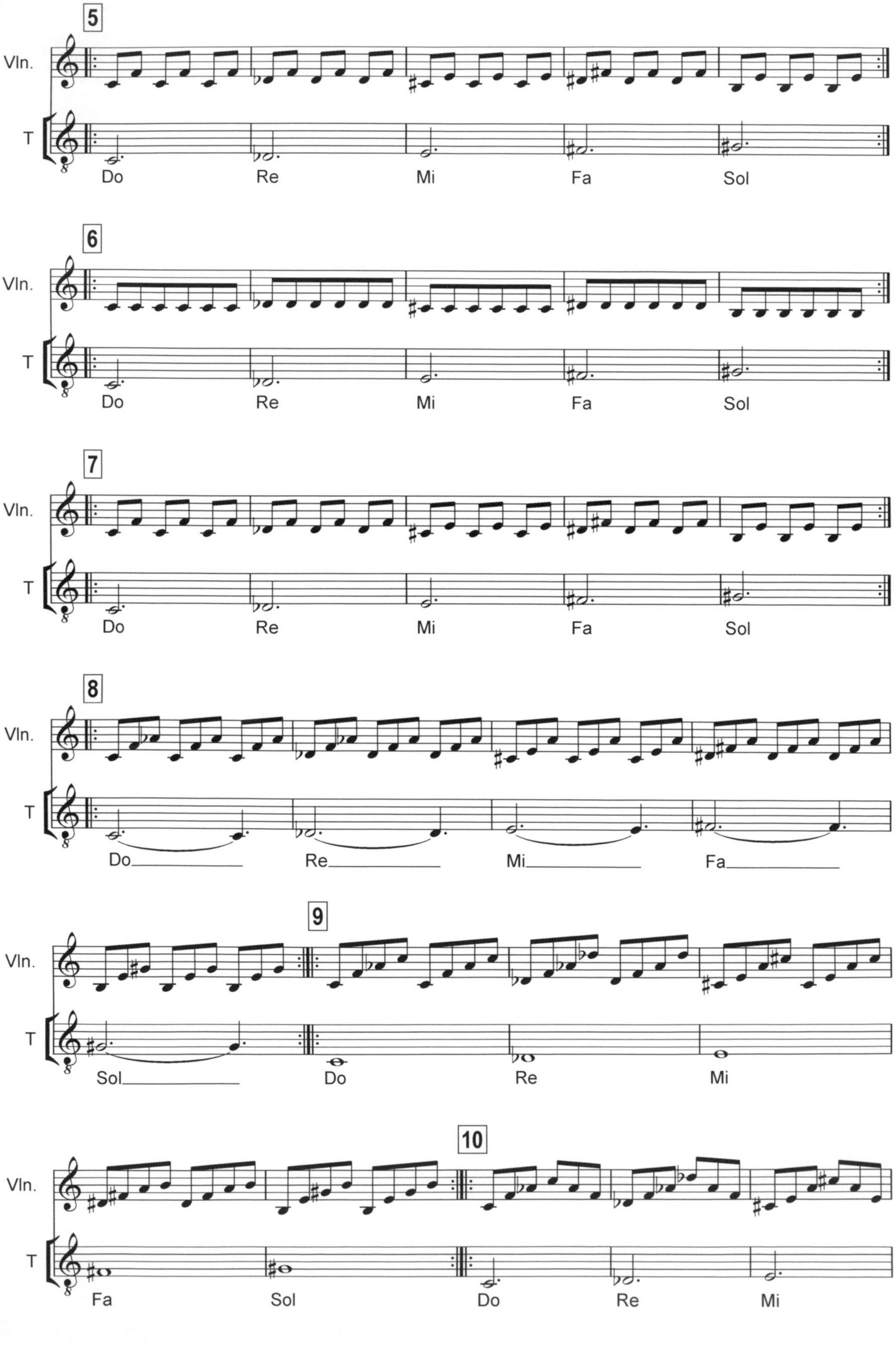
5
Vln.
T
Do Re Mi Fa Sol
6
Vln.
T
Do Re Mi Fa Sol
7
Vln.
T
Do Re Mi Fa Sol
8
Vln.
T
Do Re Mi Fa
9
Vln.
T
Sol Do Re Mi
10
Vln.
T
Fa Sol Do Re Mi

11
Vln.
T
Fa
Sol
Do
Re
Mi
Fa
Sol
12
x4
La
Si
Do
Mi
B
Mi
Sol
Mi
13
x4
La
Si
Do
Mi
Mi
Sol
Mi
14
x4
La
Si
Do
Mi
Mi
Sol
Mi

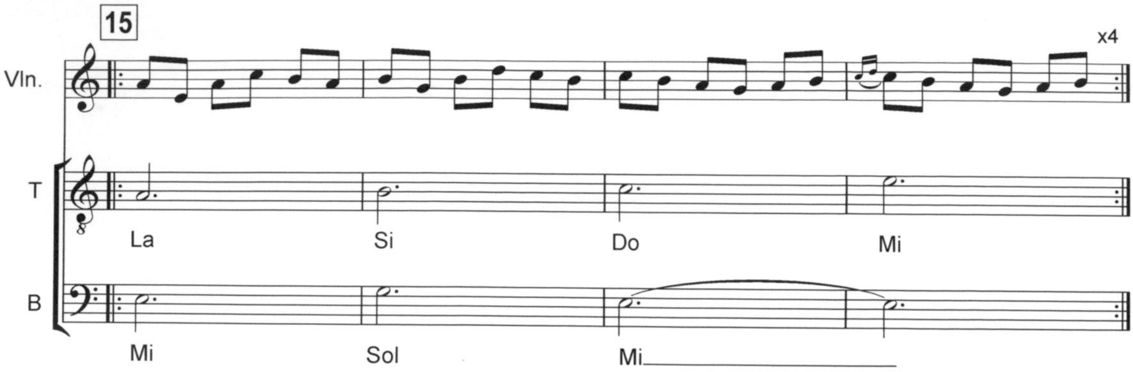
15
x4
Vln.
T
B
La
Si
Do
Mi
Mi
Sol
Mi

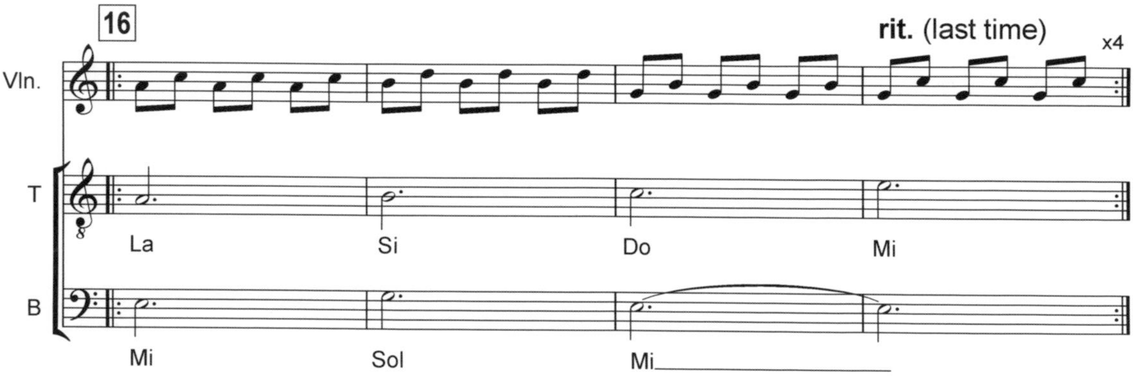
16
rit. (last time)
x4
Vln.
T
B
La
Si
Do
Mi
Mi
Sol
Mi

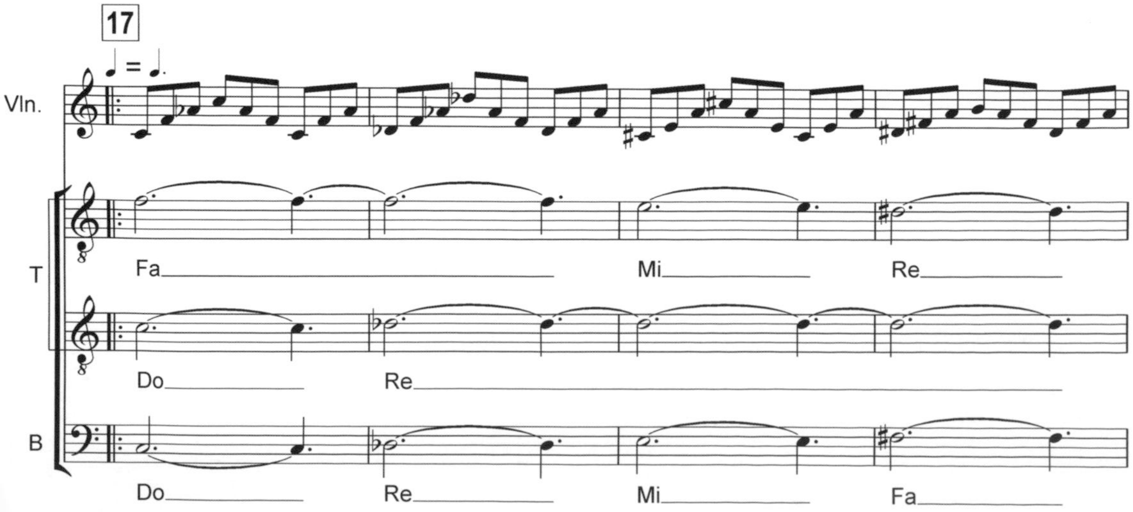
17
Vln.
T
B
Fa
Mi
Re
Do
Re
Do
Re
Mi
Fa

18
Vln.
T
B
Mi
Fa
Mi
Si
Do
Re
Sol
Do
Re
Mi
19
Vln.
Re
Mi
Fa
Si
Do
Re
T
B
Fa
Sol
Do
Re
Vln.
Mi
Re
Mi
T
Si
B
Mi
Fa
Sol

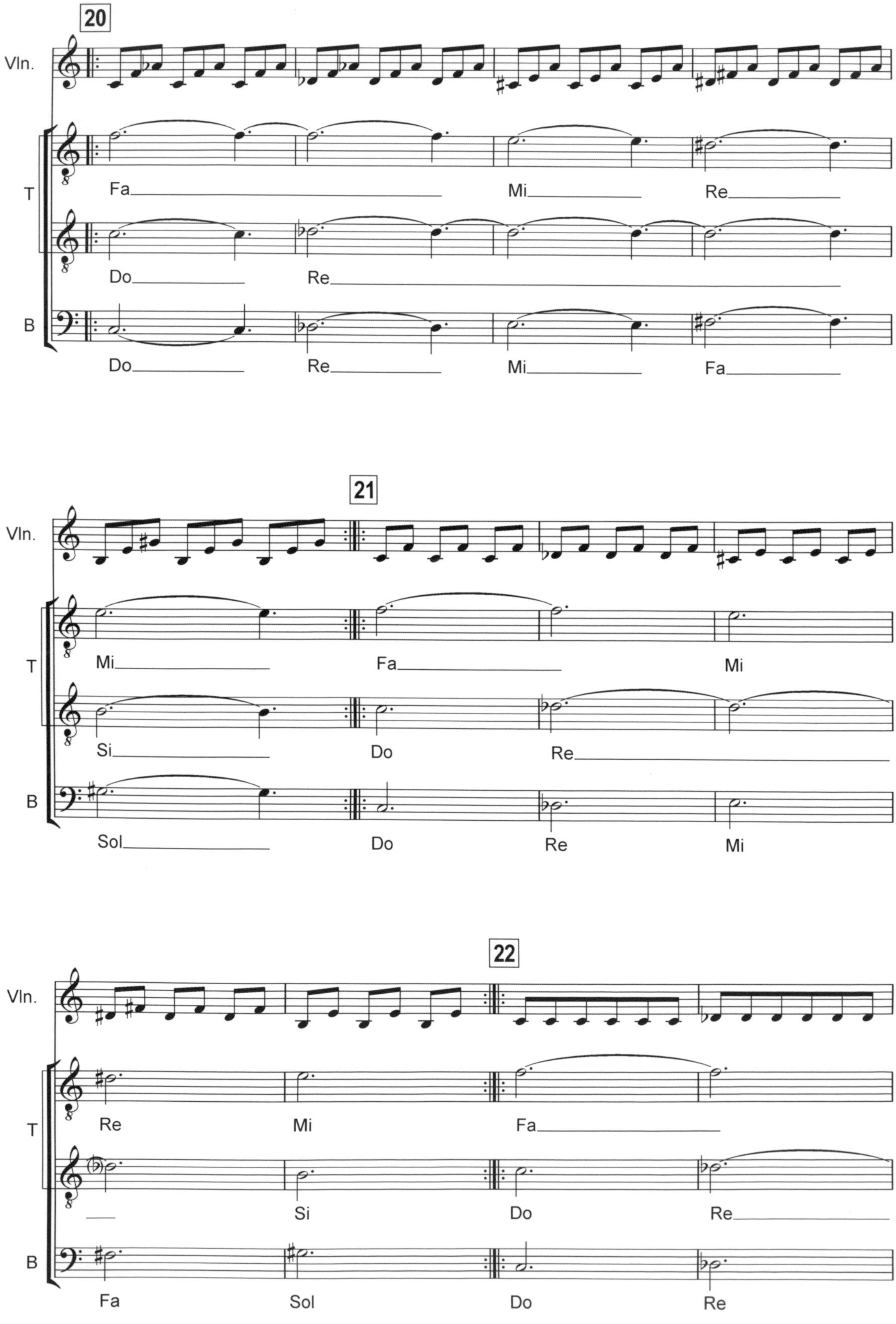
20
Vln.
T
Fa
Mi
Re
Do
Re
B
Do
Re
Mi
Fa
21
Vln.
T
Mi
Fa
Mi
Si
Do
Re
B
Sol
Do
Re
Mi
22
Vln.
T
Re
Mi
Fa
Si
Do
Re
B
Fa
Sol
Do
Re

Vln.
T
B
Mi Re Mi
Si
Mi Fa Sol
23
x4
Vln.
T
La Si Do Mi
B
Mi Sol Mi
24
x4
Vln.
T
La Si Do Mi
B
Mi Sol Mi
25
x4
Vln.
T
La Si Do Mi
B
Mi Sol Mi

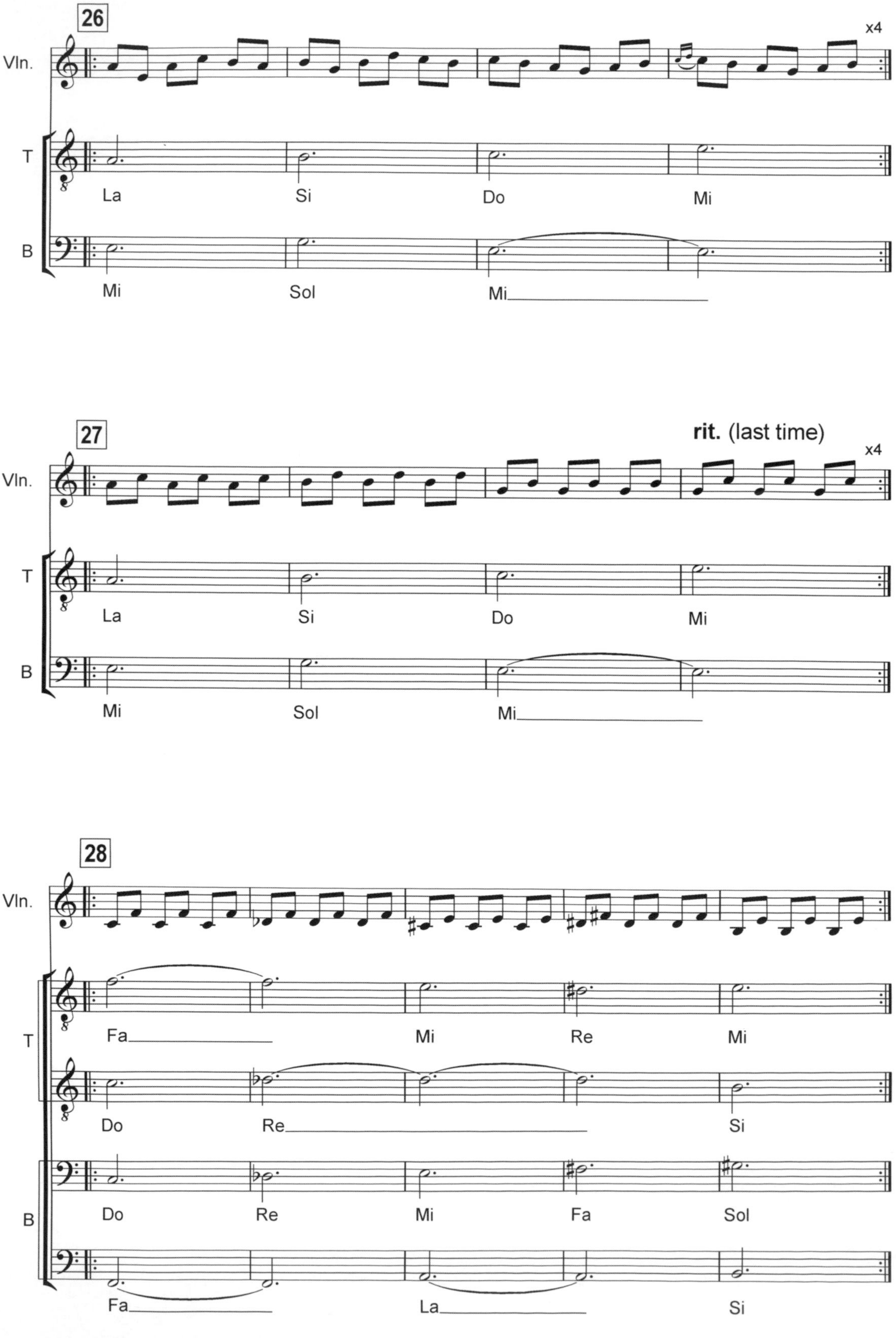
26
x4
Vln.
T
La Si Do Mi
B
Mi Sol Mi
27
rit. (last time)
x4
Vln.
T
La Si Do Mi
B
Mi Sol Mi
28
Vln.
T
Fa Mi Re Mi
Do Re Si
B
Do Re Mi Fa Sol
Fa La Si

29
Vln.
T
B
Fa
Mi
Re
Do
Re
Do
Re
Mi
Fa
Fa
La
30
Vln.
Mi
Fa
Si
Do
Re
Sol
Do
Re
Si
Fa
Vln.
Mi
Re
Mi
Si
Mi
Fa
Sol
La
Si

31
Vln.
T
Fa
Mi
Re
Do
Re
B
Do
Re
Mi
Fa
Fa
La
32
Vln.
T
Mi
Fa
Si
Do
Re
B
Sol
Do
Re
Si
Fa
Vln.
T
Mi
Re
Mi
Si
B
Mi
Fa
Sol
La
Si

Knee Play 5

Philip Glass

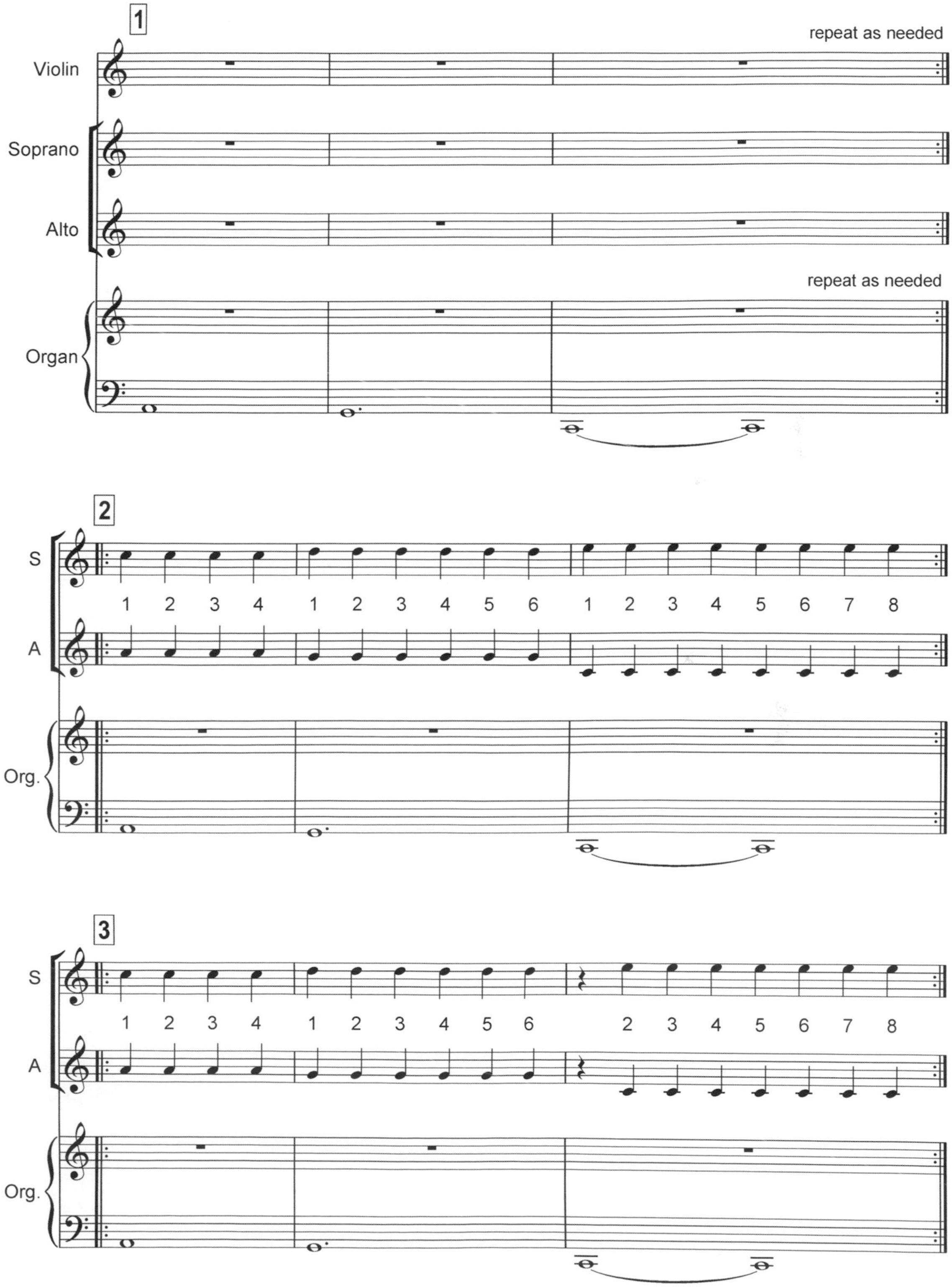

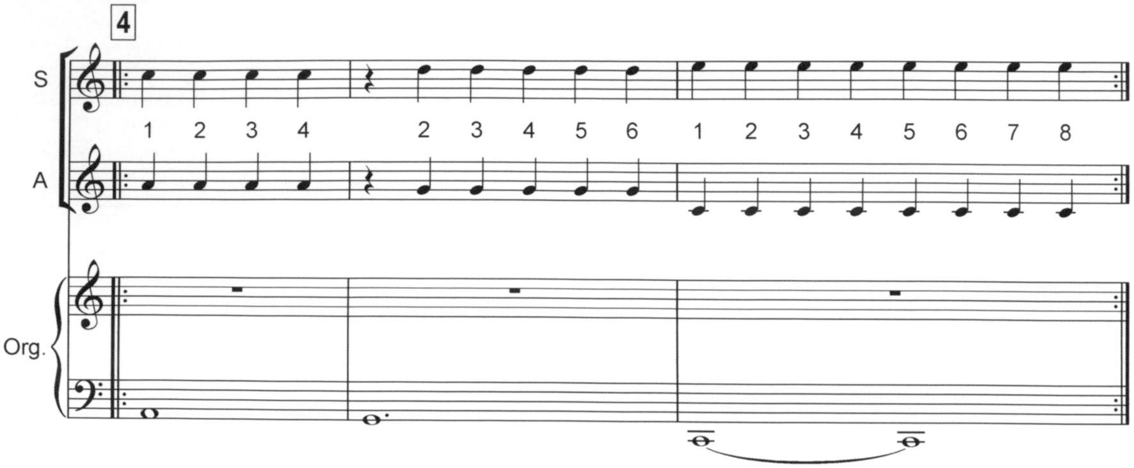
4
S
1 2 3 4 2 3 4 5 6 1 2 3 4 5 6 7 8
A
Org.

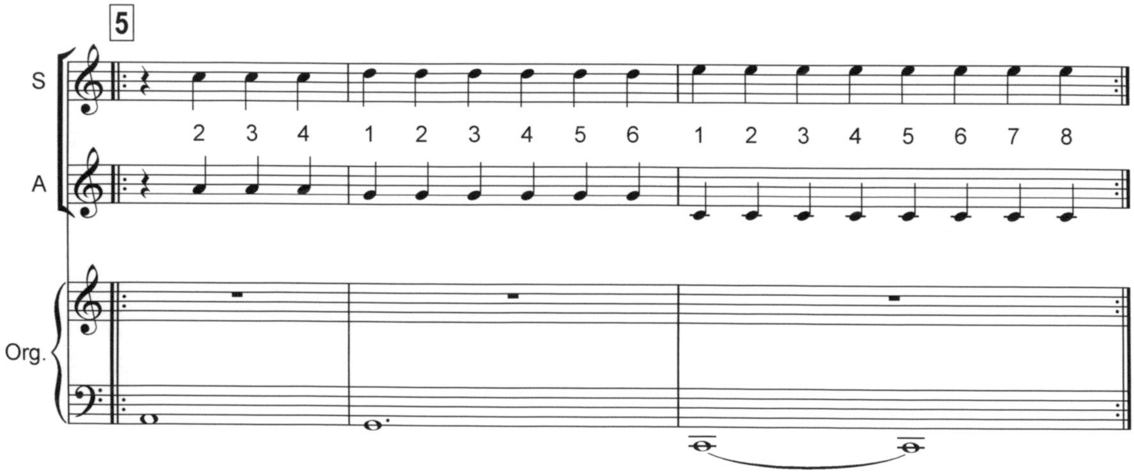
5
S
2 3 4 1 2 3 4 5 6 1 2 3 4 5 6 7 8
A
Org.

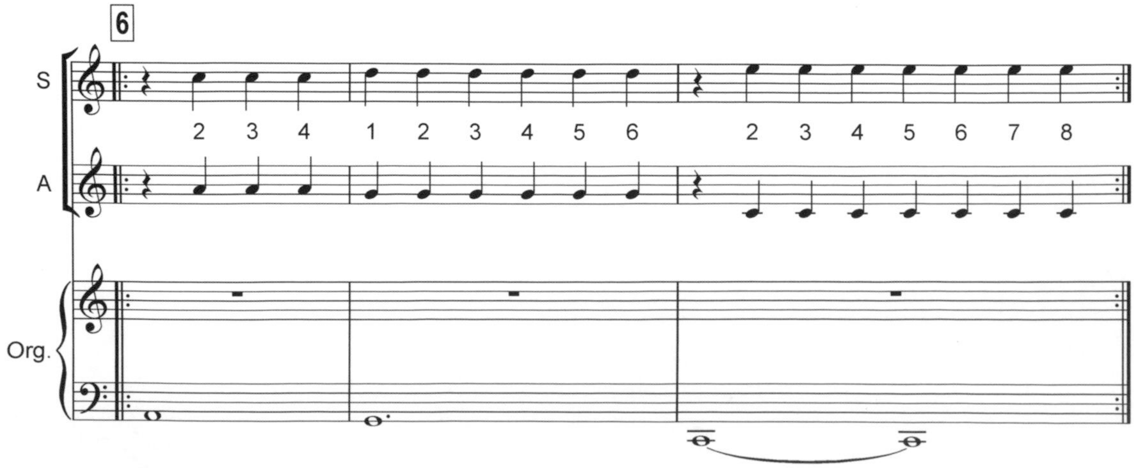
6
S
2 3 4 1 2 3 4 5 6 2 3 4 5 6 7 8
A
Org.

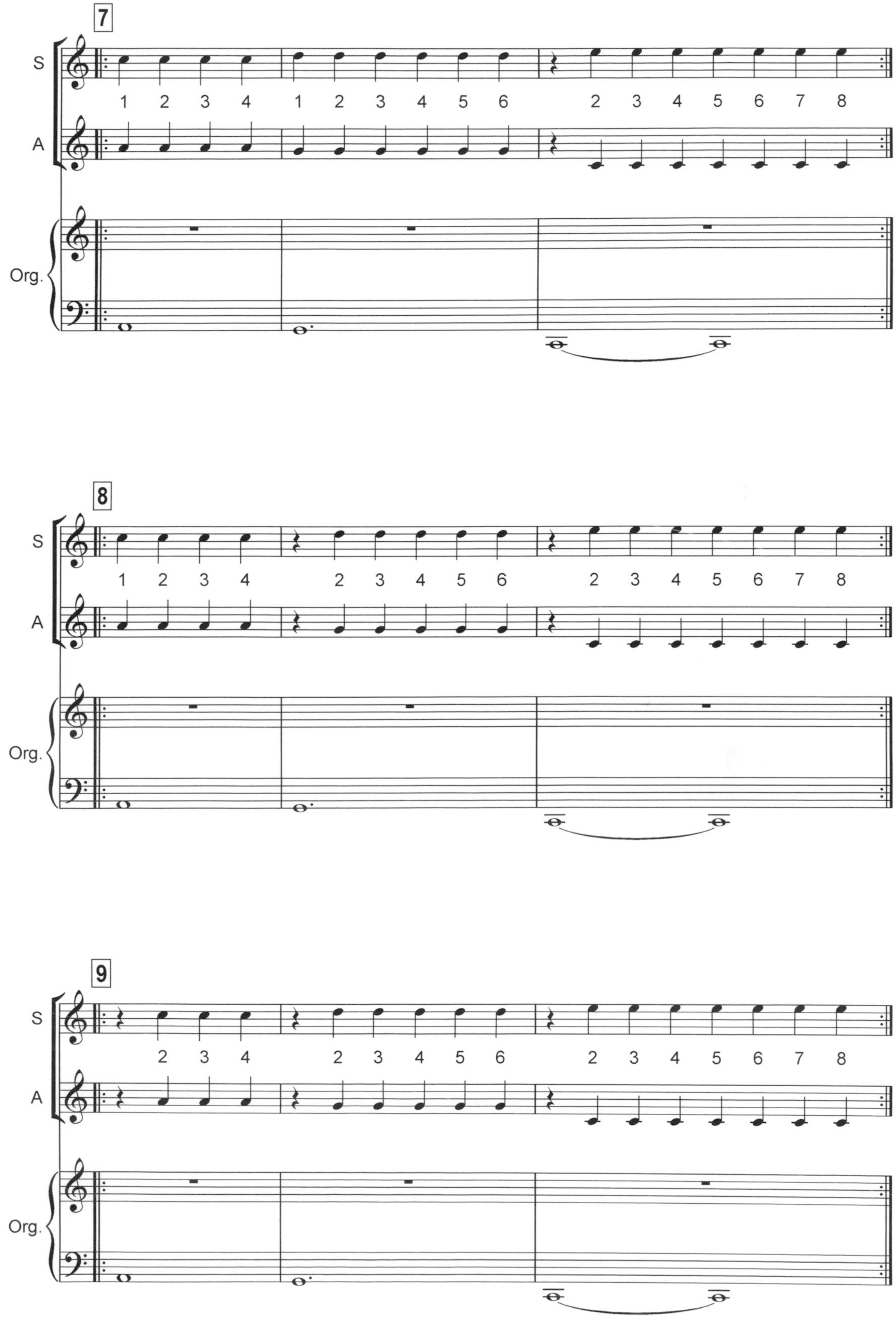
7
S
1 2 3 4 1 2 3 4 5 6 2 3 4 5 6 7 8
A
Org.
8
S
1 2 3 4 2 3 4 5 6 2 3 4 5 6 7 8
A
Org.
9
S
2 3 4 2 3 4 5 6 2 3 4 5 6 7 8
A
Org.

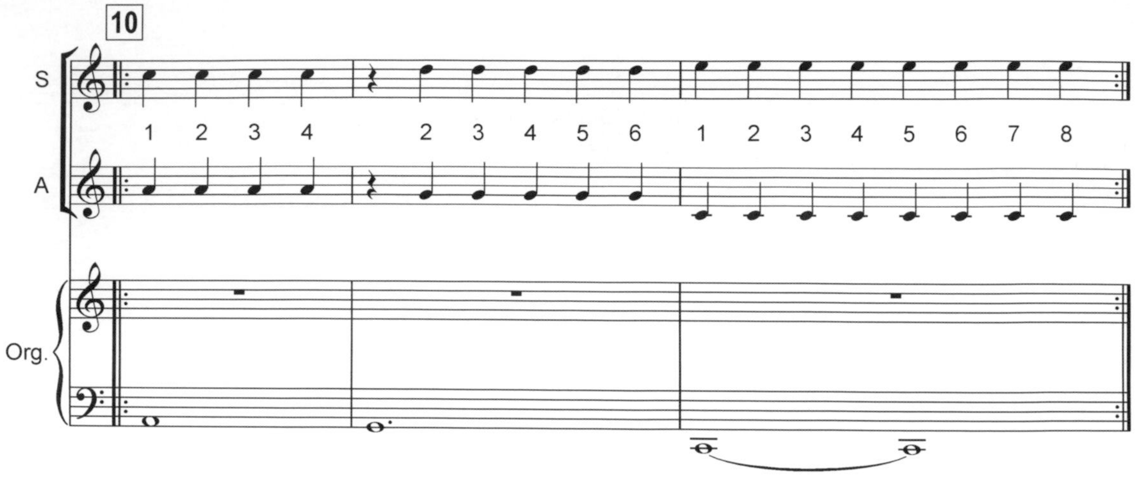
10
S
1 2 3 4 2 3 4 5 6 1 2 3 4 5 6 7 8
A
Org.

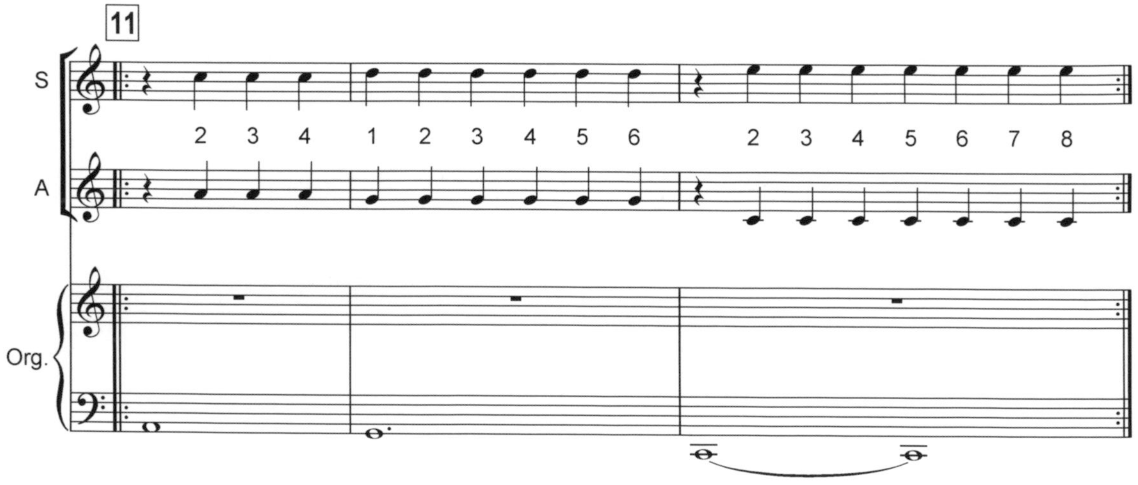
11
S
2 3 4 1 2 3 4 5 6 2 3 4 5 6 7 8
A
Org.

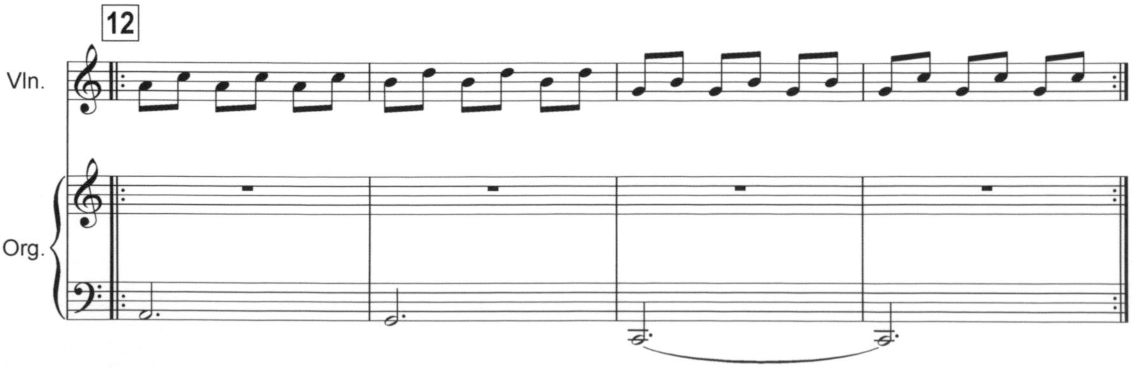
12
Vln.
Org.

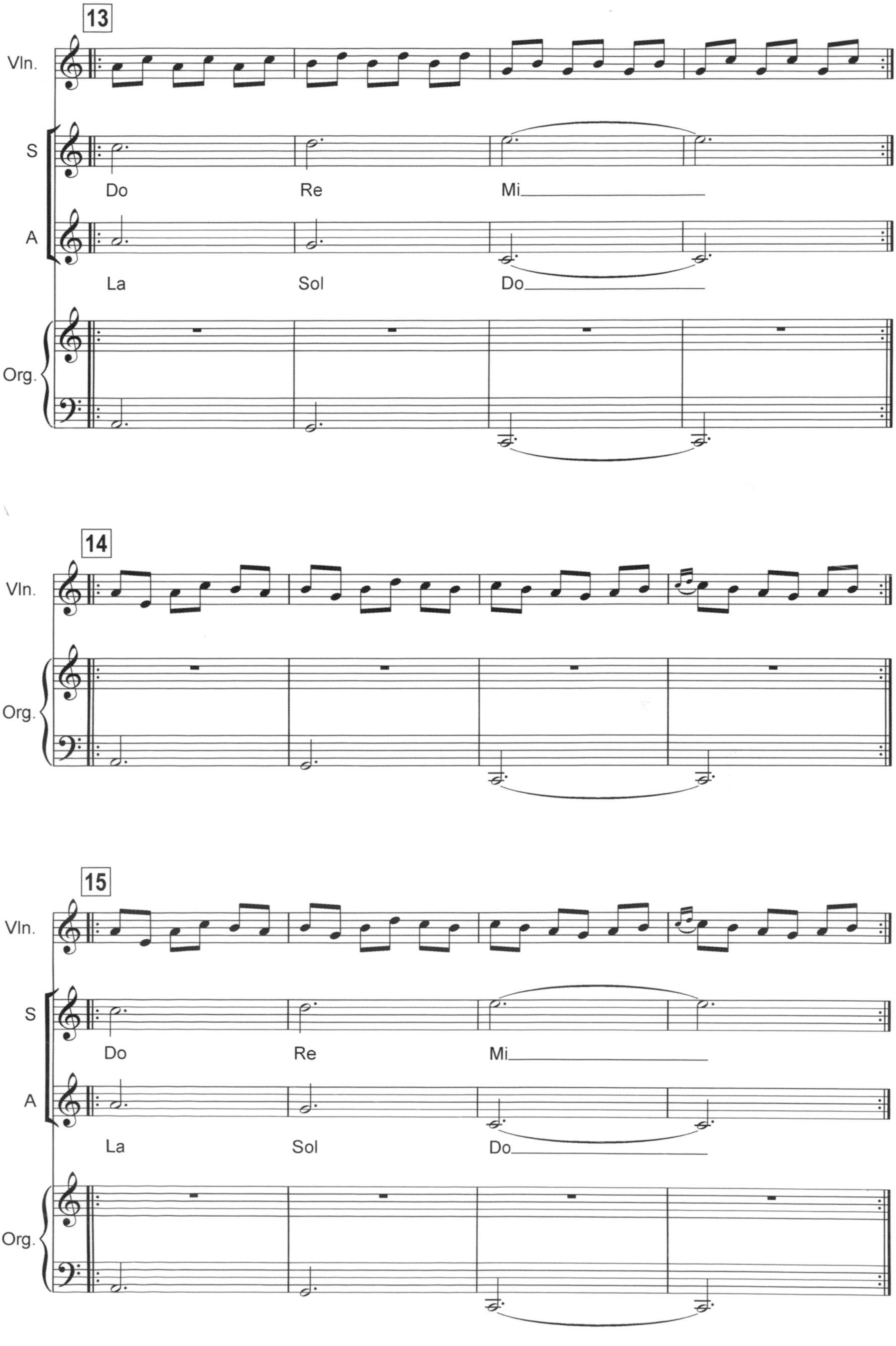
13
Vln.
S
Do
Re
Mi
A
La
Sol
Do
Org.
14
Vln.
Org.
15
Vln.
S
Do
Re
Mi
A
La
Sol
Do
Org.

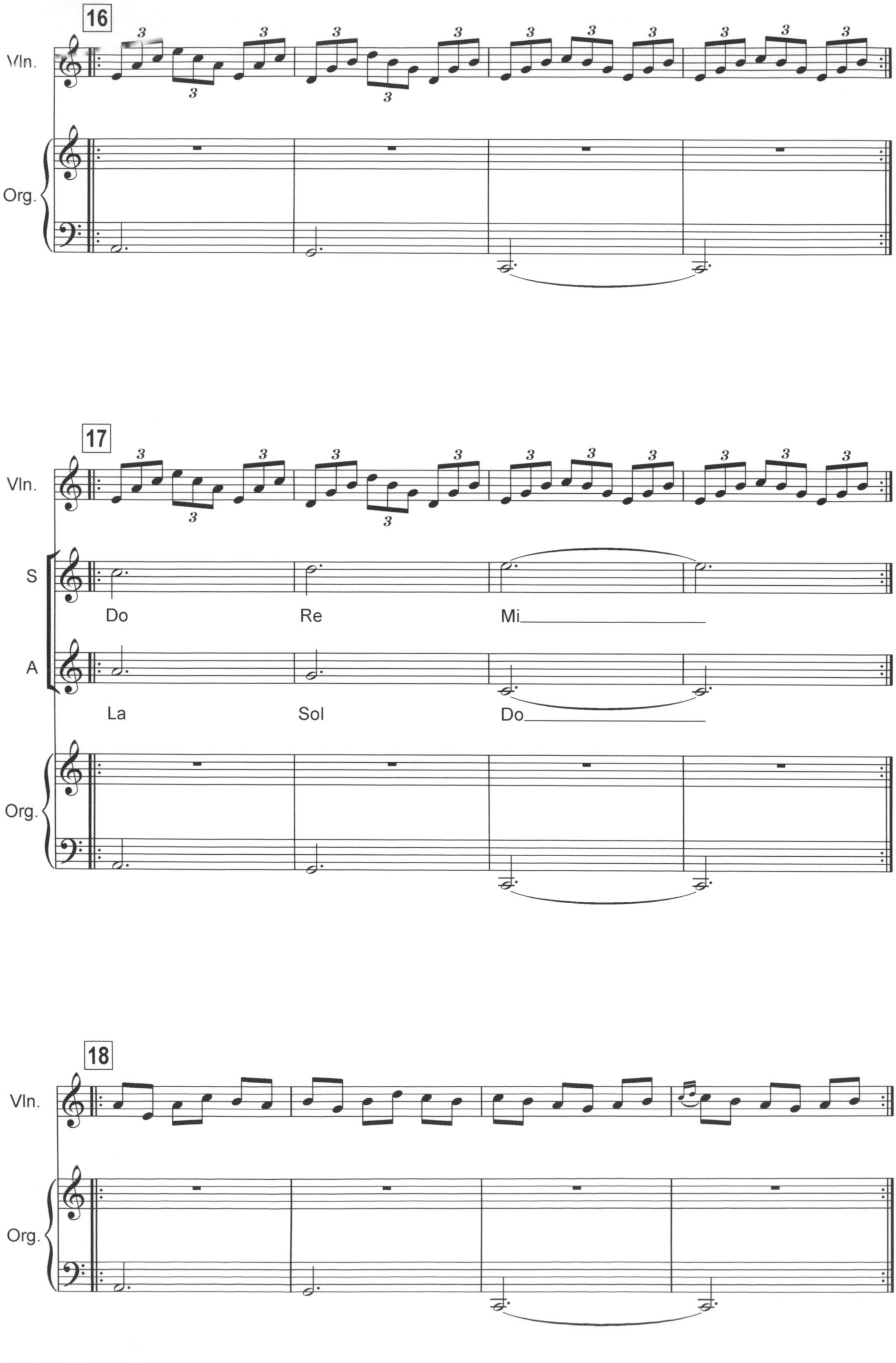
16
Vln.
Org.
17
Vln.
S
Do
Re
Mi
A
La
Sol
Do
Org.
18
Vln.
Org.

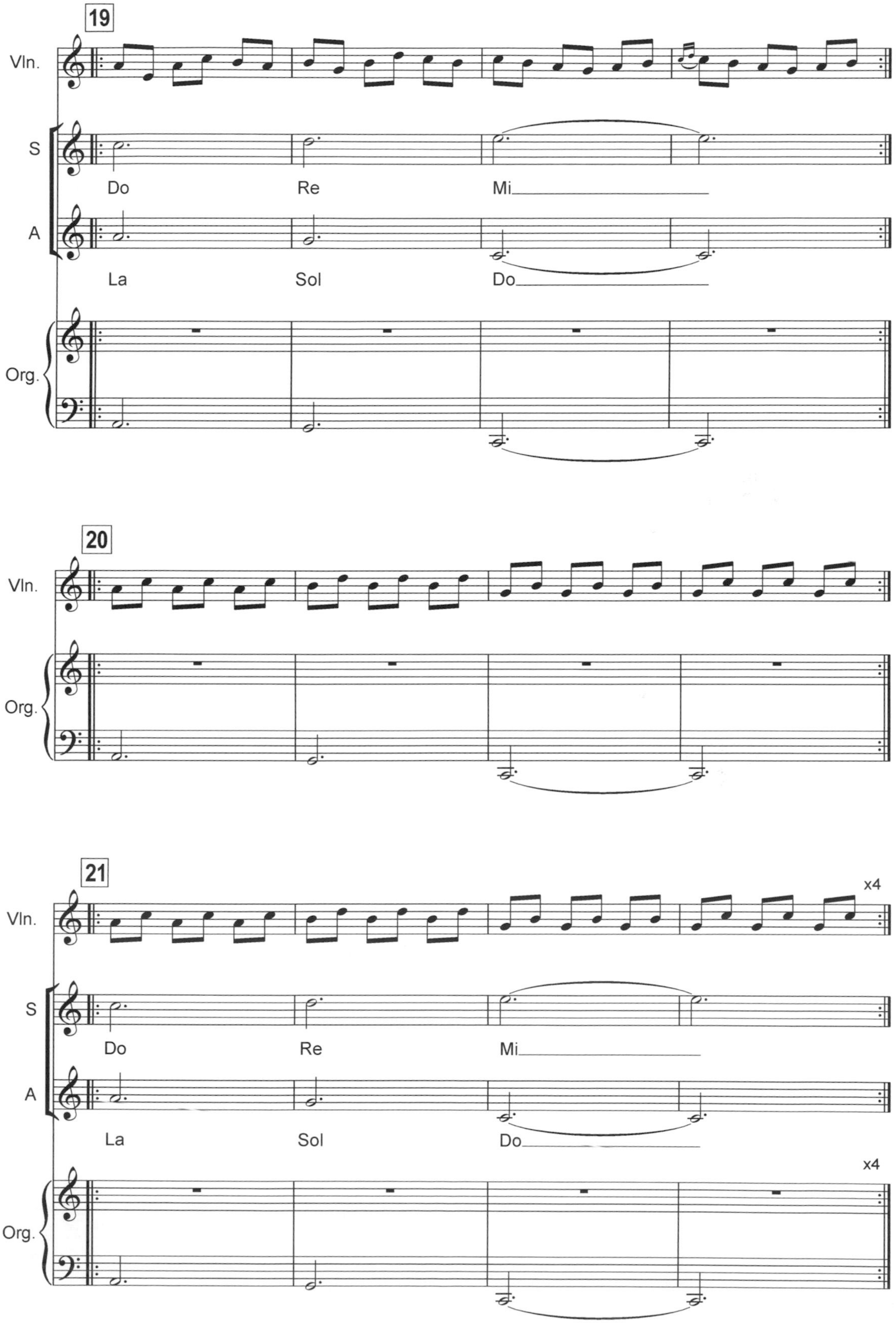
19
Vln.
S
Do
Re
Mi
A
La
Sol
Do
Org.
20
Vln.
Org.
21
x4
Vln.
S
Do
Re
Mi
A
La
Sol
Do
x4
Org.